HOW A CUP OF MASALA TEA CHANGED MY LIFE

SYDNEY FRYMIRE

Cover Image by Jesse White
http://jessewhiteillustration.com/

Contents

Prologue

When people hear about my socially conscious treks and tours to Nepal, I'm often asked, "How did you ever start? Where did the idea come from?" To begin with, I wasn't famous, didn't have a wealthy husband or a trust fund. The first time I was presented with traveling to Nepal, I couldn't imagine how I'd ever get there, or how I'd overcome my fears about leaving my well-established comfort zone.

A few months before my 50th birthday, I wanted to break out of my shell and challenge myself with something new. After I returned from that first trip in 2000, and every trip that followed, I felt energized, open to possibilities, more confident, optimistic, and filled with new ideas. The result was that I created an opportunity—The Trek of Your Life (TOYL)—to give people a unique time to think about how they would like to spend the second half of their lives. I combined my skills and passion for trekking to sponsor service-oriented group tours to Nepal, where people could both participate in a personal inner and outer journey while serving others. My goal was to add meaning and purpose to whoever wished to join me by engaging them in global causes.

Socially conscious travel is the fastest-growing segment of the travel industry because people are becoming increasingly interested in wanting to understand other countries and cultures; many are yearning for a reset after our COVID years. TOYL combined the best of travel, learning about a culture, giving a few hours of service to the community travelers visit, and offering much-needed recreation and relaxation.

This book is about my journey toward and into the second half of my life. It began after my second divorce when I was nearly 50 years old, a number that has long been the stereotypical defining moment of a middle-aged crisis. I longed for more joy, more fulfillment, more connection to the world, and more involvement in something bigger than myself, while at the same time connecting to the person I thought I was.

Instead of buying a red sports car, buying expensive jewelry, or having an affair, I trekked in Nepal. Like others, I felt confused and lost as I approached that critical age. In our increasingly wired and digitally dependent culture, I felt pressured to go, go, go all the time, and felt as if I had too much to do and not enough time.

Our bodies are designed to walk about three miles per hour. Instead, most of us speed through life in cars, buses, trains and jets. Our nervous systems can't keep up with the demands of work, friends, family, and technology which is advancing faster than our nervous systems can cope with.

I didn't realize, and never would have guessed at the time, that my first trip to Nepal in 2000 was the beginning of a deeply personal and professional transformation. Since then, I've trekked in the Himalayan Mountains 16 times, have taken small groups to Nepal yearly since 2011 (except for COVID years), and have met and made friends with fascinating people from vastly different parts of the world. We've trekked in Annapurna (2011-2014), the Solu Khumbu region (2013, 2015, 2019) the Indigenous Peoples Trek/Sailung Trek (2016), Lang Tang (2017, 2018), Pikey Peak (2019), and Tsum Valley in Manaslu Conservation Area (2022).

With other groups, I worked behind the scenes to provide hope and support to students, parents, and teachers living in Dadagaun, a small village in the foothills outside of Kathmandu, and Basa Village, a remote village in the Solu Khumbu region of Nepal. We collaborated with groups from around the world to assist these warm, loving, hard-working, kind and highly appreciative individuals to improve their lives with culturally sustainable solutions. In 2014, I met people who rescue girls from human trafficking and developed a curriculum to address their needs. Ten percent of the cost of the treks is donated to these groups.

In discovering what my journey has done for me, I have since discovered how some of those who join me take that same journey and are inspired to get out of their comfort zones, take a risk, and experience the excitement of re-imagining their own lives. For health reasons, I am no longer able to do this, but I hope that learning about my journey will inspire others to take similar risks.

PART I—MY TRAVELS TO THE HIMALAYAN MOUNTAINS

Chapter 1—Life Way Before Nepal

Several factors in my earlier life contributed to my love of travel and the eventual formation of a socially conscious business in Nepal. My parents, a doctor and a stay-at-home mother, encouraged each of their five children (I'm the oldest) to get a good education, be financially responsible for ourselves, and repeatedly urged us to "broaden our horizons" by exploring the world. My father was such a successful obstetrician/gynecologist that women drove from Ohio and West Virginia for appointments with him in Pittsburgh, Pennsylvania. When I was in high school, he journeyed to Bolivia with other doctors to treat women and children in need of basic medical attention. When he returned, he was exhilarated by experiencing another culture and his work there. He talked about what he'd like to accomplish the next time he visited Bolivia. His enthusiasm and experience left an indelible impression on me. Sadly, he never had the opportunity to return.

In 1971, after I finished college, my parents encouraged me to travel to Europe for a few months with friends. In the early seventies, a round-trip ticket to Europe cost $200, and an unlimited train pass cost about $300. The money I earned from babysitting, working in retail, and walking dogs paid for the ticket, rail pass, and living expenses to travel to Europe. In Switzerland, I met two men who were taking a gap year before starting medical school and planned to work as ski-lift operators in Zermatt. After I got home, a letter arrived from them urging me to join them, and explaining there was a waitressing job waiting for me. My parents thought it would be a great experience to go.

When I arrived in Zermatt the job as a waitress was taken, and I found another one as a chambermaid in the Zermatt Hotel located in the center of the bustling ski town. I lived outside of town in a hostel with my new friends, and spent four months learning how to clean while I enjoyed skiing for free. The hostel was built at the base of the Matterhorn, the highest mountain in the Alps on the border between Switzerland and Italy. Each morning, I walked to work along a quiet trail past sheepherders with their flock and dogs. These peaceful early morning walks were a highlight in my day. My parents were right; I was skiing for free when I had time off, I traveled, and spent time with other Americans working there.

When I returned to the States, I was hired by the National Audubon Society in Washington, D.C. as an assistant to their lobbyist. Once I became comfortable with the work, I made the decision to get engaged to someone I'd known for years from Pittsburgh, a returning Peace Corps volunteer. His experiences in Tunisia, where he served, and his travels were enticing to me. It felt natural to get married at this time. I thought I'd gone as far as I could professionally, and looked forward to the possibility of having children and being a full-time mother.

During our wedding ceremony, everyone noticed my father had a slight limp as he walked me down the aisle. None of us thought anything about it. Later, I realized my father must have known he had Lou Gehrig's disease (Amyotrophic Lateral Sclerosis). This disease, named after the famous baseball player, slowly destroyed his nervous system. Once a nerve died, the muscles and organs connected to that nerve atrophied. He remained mentally acute while his body slowly wasted away. There was no cure.

Shortly after our wedding, my husband was offered a job in Tunisia on staff with Peace Corps. Before I left to live in Tunis as a Peace Corps staff wife, my father gave me a copy of the World Atlas.

Inside he wrote, "For you—the world and the universe! Love, Dad."

While living in Tunisia, I became pregnant and learned that my father was ill. When it was time for me to deliver my baby, my mother traveled to visit me, but my father was too sick to travel. While I was in the delivery room, my mother's plane arrived in Tunis and a friend met her at the airport. My son, Andrew, was born in a small clinic after a long labor. Thankfully, my mother stayed with us for nearly a month.

Later, my father's office manager told me he couldn't imagine how or why I'd have a baby, his first grandchild, in a remote, developing country, one he knew little about. In the 1970s, letters from Tunis to Pittsburgh took nearly a month to arrive. If the telephone worked, the calls were intermittent and filled with static. My father was eager to see Andrew, and I wanted to see my father. When Andy was three months old, we returned to Pittsburgh for a visit. By this time, my father could no longer walk. He was delighted to see Andy, but could only hold him in his lap for a few minutes because his arms were too weak. One afternoon, when Andy was crying before he fell asleep, my father reassured me by saying, "Don't worry, he is only exercising; he'll quiet down soon."

It was then, after that afternoon after holding Andy, that my father and I had a conversation that stayed with me. With tears in his eyes, he told me he never dreamed he would die before he was able to enjoy his retirement. One of his dreams was to go back to Bolivia to continue the work in the clinic and have another experience like the one he had while I was in high school.

The lesson he learned too late was unforgettable. Like many people, he'd postponed finding joy, excitement, and fulfillment until later in his life. How could I avoid doing that? I decided to pay attention to my gut feelings, find meaningful work, take risks, and not put off the experiences I felt passionate about. But was this, as they say, easier said than done?

Chapter 2—My Career

Fifteen months after that conversation, my father died at 62. Andy was 15 months old, and I was almost eight months pregnant with my daughter, Dana Louise. A few months before he died, we returned from Tunisia to live in Boston while my husband attended graduate school. After my father died and my husband finished graduate school, he found a job in Pittsburgh in a bank.

This was a challenging time for my new family, and I struggled to keep us together. My husband was unhappy with his job, and with me. We had couples therapy. It seemed as if I couldn't do anything the way he wanted. Trying to help, one of our friends from the Peace Corps and a trainer with Lifespring (an experiential self-growth training) encouraged us to go to Washington, D.C. to participate in the training. My husband went first and said it was a "life-changing experience." Our friend called me and insisted that I attend, too. After I took the basic training, we decided to take the next level to help us make changes in our lives. In addition to learning skills, this was the first time I got more in touch with myself, learned to get out of my comfort zone, take risks, and not let fear inhibit me.

Afterward, we moved to D.C. because my husband wanted to find a new job. We house-sat for eight weeks while he looked for work. Meanwhile, I worried about our finances and moving around with two small children, a cat and a dog, and a crib tied to the top of the small Fiat station wagon that we owned. Finally, my in-laws decided to help us by renting a small house for us in NW Washington, D.C. I found a job before my husband as a secretary, and my children attended St. Alban's childcare center. While I was working as a secretary, time seemed to crawl by and I couldn't seem to type fast or accurately. A few weeks later, my husband found a job too.

The best part of my day was returning to the childcare center to see my children and take them home. One morning when I was dropping them off, the director of the center offered me a job as an assistant teacher. I accepted on the spot, and asked if I could start in two weeks so I could give notice at my job. It was a welcome transition for me and my children.

I've always found it fascinating, sometimes strangely so, how certain paths in life begin as others end, leading in a new direction. A few years after settling in Washington, D.C., while I was engaged in conversation at a moms' soccer dinner, one of the moms walked from the other end of the long dinner table to tell me about her divorce. Her story was heartbreaking and very moving. This wasn't the first time someone sought me out to talk to me about their personal problems. It signaled something about me. I thought I might investigate how I could make a career out of listening to and guiding other people. I discovered that a master's in social work would teach a holistic systems approach to working with people. I'd learn how to think about a person in the context of their lives, family, and community. In those days, there was health insurance available to those seeking counseling.

In spite of my insecurities and doubts, I applied to The Catholic University of America in Washington, D.C., and was accepted as a provisional student since my college transcript was average; I always struggled in school. I registered as a four-year part-time student, attended classes, studied, and wrote papers while my children were in school or asleep. Feeling a sense of urgency I didn't understand at the time, I took classes during the summer, which gave me enough credits to complete my degree in three years. The day I graduated was one of the happiest days of my life.

Shortly after my graduation, my husband moved out of our home, ending our 13 years of marriage. I realized later that I'd fallen into the same trap many women fall into. I married someone well-educated, from another Pittsburgh family, but he was unstable and left for another woman. I was devastated and couldn't imagine how I was going to manage as a single parent. Not only did my children no longer have a father in their home, but I went to work full time. After three years of working as foster care social worker and earning my license, I found my first secure job with benefits as a therapist in a community mental health center for Montgomery County Government. I loved the work and was relieved that I was able to support my family, but felt torn between having to work and wanting to be at home with my children. More challenging years followed.

Andy and Dana gradually adjusted to living with a single mother working full time but struggled with feeling abandoned by their father and me. I was no longer able to attend all their activities and missed the time I used to spend with them at home. Fortunately, they had generous scholarships to a reputable private school where they received extra attention, played sports, and had lots of friends. We found time to enjoy the enriching programs at the Smithsonian Zoo, art classes, and museums in Washington, D.C.; the zoo and the Museum of Natural History became as familiar to them as their own backyard. Especially on the drizzly days when few other families went to the zoo, they'd run from one end to the other. When he became a teenager,

Andy said, "Mom, no more plays, museums, or hiking." Now, as a father, he appreciates those outings.

Life became one big juggling act between fulfilling their needs, keeping up our finances, and the demands of my job. I wanted a better life for them and remarried shortly after the divorce. Looking back, I realized I was too vulnerable at the time to choose wisely. Although it seemed like this husband was financially stable and would be a good influence on my children since he was a father and had an interest in personal growth and meditation, I made what was, unfortunately, a typical mistake for a woman in my position in the eighties. He was conflicted about being married and was unhappy about it; we went to marriage counseling together and I started individual therapy. My husband and I attended meditation groups and workshops conducted by teachers from India. Nothing seemed to help. After three years, he moved out and we got divorced.

As a therapist, I found my relationships with colleagues provided structure and support. Several of us became friends and practiced meditation with a spiritual teacher from India. As a group, we traveled to her ashram in upstate New York for weekend retreats many times. At these retreats, I learned practices based on energy and Ayurvedic medicine, meditation, and mindfulness practices to enhance my daily life.

During that time, memories of childhood sexual abuse by my father surfaced. Fortunately, Diane Koslow, my therapist, had training and experience with incest survivors. I realized that if I didn't face what had happened to me, my children would suffer more than they already were suffering. She continued to guide me and encouraged me for many years to take intensives at the ashram, participate in a two-year training program with Rudy Bauer at the Washington Conscious Center, and trek in Nepal.

Facing another divorce after just a few years left me overwhelmed. To supplement my income, I started a private practice in 1998 and saw clients Saturday mornings and Mondays-Fridays before and after I went to my county job. My life was structured around spending as much time as I could at home, keeping track of teenagers, and working. It seemed like a miracle to me that I could juggle it all.

Our beloved family pets, Harley (a black Lab mix, the only Harley my son would ever get), TJ (a one hundred 15-pound Lab-Chesapeake Golden Retriever mix), and Dusty (a grey Himalayan mixed cat) were lifelines for us. Our time together walking them and taking care of them added joy to our lives and helped sustain our family life.

After my daughter started college, I attended a seven-day intensive at the ashram on Kundalini energy. This led me to Synergy Dance classes based on Polarity Therapy and Ayurvedic medicine, where I learned about the interdependence of body, mind, and spirit, and the value of creating a way of life in harmony with nature. Again, I was fortunate to have a master trainer and teacher, Charmaine Lee, the founder of Synergy Dance.

These modalities that seemed to enter my life on their own led me in the direction of a dream I never knew I wanted. I hadn't traveled for years but decided to visit my son for parents' weekend at the University of Colorado in Boulder. Back in those days, there were no TVs or internet on the planes, just magazines. The only one available was *Sports Illustrated*, which I had no interest in reading. I picked it up anyway and happened to open it to an article about trekking in Nepal. I was entranced by the author's description of his trek, the culture, the people, and the mountains. In the breathtaking scenery while camping, he wrote about being served a cup of masala tea in his tent in the mornings. Just the thought of going to a remote, exotic culture, and being served a warm cup of masala tea by the cook's assistant upon awakening seemed magical. Later, I learned masala tea, also called sherpa tea, is black tea with hot milk, cinnamon, cardamom, cloves, ginger and sugar.

Rationally, I couldn't imagine how I would go on a remote trip like that. I didn't have money, time, or even know where Nepal was, but was so excited by the idea. I remembered my spiritual teacher who encouraged her students to travel where they felt drawn. Something, she said, would unfold for us there, and I wanted to do something big. This trip would be a gift to myself for my 50th birthday. It was time for an adventure.

Soon after I returned from Colorado, I met an international management consultant at a brunch. When I asked him, "What is your favorite country in the world?" He replied, "Nepal." He had just returned from trekking the Annapurna Circuit. Coincidental? Not really. As we continued our conversation, he offered to send me information about who to travel with, what to take, and how to get there. Later, he made lists for me, helped me shop for hiking boots, socks, hiking skirts and long underwear, and he shared my excitement.

I registered for a 21-day trek organized by Wilderness Travel in Nepal's Annapurna Range; but when I asked my boss for a month off from work, he told me it was too much time, and others never requested that much time for a trip. After I pointed out the number of annual leave days I had accrued, he reluctantly signed my leave slip. My colleagues warned me I'd lose clients in my private practice. My friends' reactions to my going were surprising. None were interested in traveling with me; most faces went blank and their eyes glazed over. Others would light up and say, "I've always wanted to go to Nepal," but wouldn't join me. I found this perplexing.

Several months before my trip, my daughter invited me to go out to dinner with her best friend and her parents. Making small talk at dinner, I said, "I'm planning to go trekking in Nepal in a few months. My friends all think I'm crazy, so I'm going by myself with a group organized by Wilderness Travel." My daughter's friend's mother, whom I had just met for the first time, looked at me, raised her hand, and said, "I'll go with you." I was delighted. Her husband was taken aback and offered to hire extra porters for us; he couldn't imagine how we'd manage. Since he and his wife lived on Long Island, New York, we decided to travel separately and meet in the Shangri-La Hotel in Kathmandu. Our daughters thought it was cool we were going. They gave each of us headlights to wear at night in our tents.

To get in shape for the trek, I started to hike with the Sierra Club and on trails near my house in Bethesda, Maryland. Then the mishaps began. One Saturday, I got up early to meet a hiking group, but completely missed the hike because I couldn't find the meeting place. I felt so discouraged and disheartened, that I went home to get back in bed wondering why I ever thought I could trek in Nepal if I couldn't even find a hike nearby in Maryland.

Then, a month before I left, my right foot started to hurt. A podiatrist told me I had a neuroma, a pinched nerve, and needed surgery. This was out of the question. He gave me an insert for my boot and told me it would help. Then, days before my departure, I was rushing back to my office, completely missed a curb, and fell all the way down on the street. Why had I ever thought I could trek in the Himalayas? I was consumed with so many doubts and arrangements for being out of the country, I barely thought about what might happen when I got there. My children were simultaneously excited and worried.

Chapter 3—The Annapurna Sanctuary Trek: 25 days, including 14-Day Moderate-to-Rigorous Trek, October 8-29, 2000

Somehow, I got on the plane. The trip from the States through Bangkok, Thailand to Kathmandu took over 38 hours. The 4-hour flight from Bangkok, which suddenly dropped into Kathmandu Valley in between the tallest mountains in the world, was thrilling to me. When I got off the plane, I felt exhilarated at seeing these majestic mountains, yet exhausted from the long flight and jet lag. As I made my way through a sea of unfamiliar faces at the airport, I was relieved to see a Wilderness Travel agent holding a sign above her head with my name on it. We drove in a car to the hotel through narrow crowded chaotic streets filled with traffic, motorcycles, people, wandering cows, rickshaws, street dogs, vendors, bicycles, carts, flowers, and the brightest blues, yellows, and orange colors I'd ever seen. Motorcycles and cars honked. Rickshaw bells rang. The air smelled of wood burning, kerosene, incense, flowers, and exhaust from cars. As we inched through traffic we passed Buddhist monks of all ages, women in brightly colored saris, merchants, marigold sellers, children playing jacks with stones, grandparents holding children, government workers, tourists, guides, and sherpas with trekkers. My guide casually explained that we had to make a slight detour because there was a political incident in one of the neighborhoods on the way. I was oblivious to the fact that the country was on the brink of a civil war.

At Hotel Shangri-La I stepped into a serene and quiet world with a beautiful back garden and lovely pool. A host welcomed me with a warm smile and handed me a refreshing glass of fruit juice served on a brass tray. Kindness, ritual, and respect seemed interwoven into every gesture of each Nepalese person I met. If I had a question or needed something, everyone was genuinely pleased to go out of their way to help. Their warmth and kindness touched my heart.

Orientation for our group of four was given by Kathy Butler, our trek leader. She impressed us with her cultural sensitivity and knowledge of Nepal. She had been living in Kathmandu for 15 years, was trained as a nurse, and had experience trekking in Russia, Pakistan, Mongolia, Bhutan, China, India and Tibet. She urged us to wear our trekking skirts to show respect, as the women in Nepal wear saris or Tibetan clothes, asked us to burn or carry out any toilet paper we used, not to use aerosol cans while trekking, and to be careful not to talk about money with our staff. To the Nepalese, spending $10 on snacks would seem like an enormous amount of money and be confusing for them. She explained that Nepal was her favorite country because she loved the Nepalese people for their generous spirits and simple kindness. She concluded her talk and said, "Something unexpected always happens in Nepal."

Before we began our trek, we spent our first two days touring UNESCO World Heritage sites in Kathmandu. Our tour guide, hired for the day, explained that politically, Nepal is like a goat between a dragon (China) and a tiger (India). Hinduism is the state religion of Nepal and is interwoven with Buddhism, the religion of nearly one-third of the Nepalese today. Many animistic religions, Buddhism, Hinduism, Islam, and Christianity are practiced in Nepal, resulting in great tolerance and friendliness in the local people.[1] They believe they are living in the lap of the Gods. The rich cultural heritage of the Kathmandu Valley is illustrated by seven groups of monuments and buildings, Durbar Squares, which display the full range of historic and artistic achievements for which the Kathmandu Valley is world famous.[2]

---

[1]The Himalayas, Texts and Photographs: Alain Cheneviere, p.113, Konecky & Konecky, New York, New York, 1998

[2]2 Ibid, Cheneviere, introduction p.15

Centuries ago, Kathmandu Valley consisted of small kingdoms. In 1979, the Durbar Square in each city was designated a UNESCO World Heritage Site. Durbar Square is the generic name used to describe plazas and areas opposite the old royal palaces in Nepal, which are the most prominent remnants of those old kingdoms before reunification. Each of these treasures once defined the valley's peak of power and beauty. The three most famous, belonging to the three Newar kingdoms are Kathmandu Durbar Square, Patan Durbar Square, and Bhaktapur Durbar Square. Each has temples, idols, open courts, and water fountains restored and overseen by the Kathmandu Valley Preservation Trust and other nonprofits.[3] The side streets and winding medieval streets were busy, colorful, and peaceful compared to the main streets.

We toured these intriguing sites, including Hanuman Dhoka (Durbar Square in Kathmandu), the Buddhist stupas of Swayambhu Maha Chaitya (Monkey Temple), Boudhanath (Buddhist temple), and the Hindu temple of Pashupatinath, Nepal's most sacred Hindu shrine and one of the subcontinent's greatest Shiva sites, actually a sprawling collection of temples, ashrams, images and inscriptions raised over the centuries along the banks of the sacred

---

[3]http://en.wikipedia.org/wiki/Durbar_Square Page

Bagmati River. I remember a conversation I had with our tour guide as we gazed at holy men on the grounds across the river from Pashupatinath. Naively, I told him about the guru I followed and was humbled by his response. He looked at me kindly, smiled, and said, "The gurus who travel West know how to present it for you, don't they? The experience you are about to have will be a very different kind of spiritual journey."

On the third day we set off, ready to trek, after a 35-minute plane trip to Pokhara, the departure town for all the treks in the region. I was in a daze. Our guides and staff met us at the airport, organized our bags, and loaded us into a van. We drove an hour or so to where we began our trek. As we began, Kathy and our guide made it a point to remind us that the weather in the Annapurna Range—really, anywhere in the mountains—can change instantly. I snuck a look at my fellow trekkers. Did any of them feel the small alarm that I did? Why did Kathy bring this up again so specifically? She also informed us that behind the scenes, the trekking staff performed pujas (rituals involving offerings to the gods) for a safe, successful trek. All my subsequent treks included pujas too.

Then we proceeded to walk on footpaths and up countless stone steps that had been used for centuries in an area with no electricity or running water. We were completely unplugged. While our porters carried sleeping bags, tents, folding tables and chairs, food, and cooking utensils, we carried our day packs with water, snacks, cameras, rain gear, and toilet paper with a lighter to burn it after use. Have you ever tried burning wet toilet paper? I tried once and have never tried again.

After a few hours of watching us hike, Kathy gave a lesson on walking. She demonstrated standing erect instead of leaning forward from our waists as we climbed up steep inclines, encouraging us to walk much slower and take "proper breaks," as she called them. This meant taking off our packs, sitting down, drinking water, and having a snack. In the long run, we'd feel better.

We began our trek at Thare Khola, a stream bed that was dry that time of year. Our route climbed up steeply along the west bank of the stream, then traversed through farmland and Hindu villages. When we stopped for lunch, my new friend worried that she hadn't trained enough for our trek. We'd never walked up so many steps for so long, and we were still in the foothills. Our reward came when we reached Bhumdi for our first night of camping, and the grand view of Machapuchare ("Fishtail") and the Annapurnas. Each of the campsites for the rest of the trek was set up in similar spots, each offering breathtaking views of the mountains. Several mornings, our dining table was set up outside so we could enjoy the view.

Since each group member walked at a different pace, we spread out along the trail. Once I learned to focus on taking one step at a time, my breathing and the beauty surrounding us, I began to experience deep serenity and felt carefree. It became easy to lose myself in the rhythm of walking while I listened to my hiking poles click when they touched the ground and the soft joyful voices of the two guides behind the group. Often, they sang folk songs as they walked along the trail. When my feet hurt and I thought I was too exhausted to take one more step, my friend reminded me cheerfully, "Sydney, just look around you. See where we are!" It didn't take long before my aching feet started to develop blisters. Every time we stopped for a break, I took my boots off to stretch my toes. Eventually, Kathy gave me duct tape to wrap around my feet to protect them from developing more blisters. It worked like magic. Good old duct tape— never leave home without it.

We hiked on ridge trails, climbed up through lush deciduous forests full of bird life, tree orchids, rhododendrons, and open grassy areas, and ascended along the Modi Khola River Valley. This glacial river, the clearest jade color I'd ever seen, drains the Annapurna Sanctuary. The mountains were luminous.

Along the way, our guides pointed out hanging lichen, varieties of moss, ferns, rhododendrons, orchids, white mycelia, and fields of golden barley and rice. Trains of ponies and burros passed us carrying heavy loads of rice and supplies. The padding of their hooves, accompanied by the soft sound of the bells hanging around their necks, created a mystical environment for us. The sounds of nature and the scent of incense and flowers were intoxicating. I'd never before experienced anything like it.

Occasionally, Kathy led us off the well-worn path through villages to visit temples tourists typically didn't have the opportunity to visit. She introduced us to local gurus who sat in small rustic temples, and we saw caves where monks practiced their meditation for decades. In one, the energy was overpowering. I sat there for as long as time allowed. Afterward, I started to feel dizzy and nauseated. Soon, I was vomiting over stone walls and felt weak. Kathy convinced me to take an antibiotic, Cipro. I felt well by the next day. It is hard to prove, but I wonder if I experienced a "spiritual cleansing"? It seemed like it.

Visiting these temples and walking at less than two miles per hour at about an altitude of 8,000 to 11,000 feet, I began to understand how spiritual journeys, pre-airline and pre-car, were as important as reaching a destination. Walking one day after another along trails that were considered sacred, gazing at the grandeur around me, and camping, left us feeling like were in a trance. When I asked Kathy, "How many miles did we walk?" She replied, "The changes in altitude and hiking up and down make distance irrelevant." Nowadays, group members have fit bits which allow them to track mileage and altitude. She and the guides were exquisitely attuned to us, closely watching to make sure we ate enough power bars on the trail and were fully hydrated by drinking nearly four quarts of water each day to keep ourselves fortified and acclimatized.

After eight days of trekking, we met stunning panoramic views of the Annapurna Range. I'd seen the Matterhorn, been to Colorado and other western states, including the Bridger Wilderness in Wyoming, and seen pictures of other mountains, of course. But never before had I experienced mountains like these, with nothing between us but air. It seemed like we could touch them. Annapurna I (26,545'), the sacred "fishtail" spire of Machapuchare (22,943') and other giants formed a mountain-ringed amphitheater around our campsites. After a long, unusually hot day of hiking, we camped in the Annapurna Sanctuary itself, a huge glacial circuit of mountains about 23,000' high, and refreshed ourselves with a brief swim in the freezing river near camp.

The Himalayas, the youngest, tallest, and greatest mountains in the world, bear the stamp of the infinite. Only superlatives can begin to describe them. Named the "Roof of the World," they are the result of two tectonic plates crashing into each other centuries ago, and are still growing. Each time I saw them, I was awed by how sharp and well-defined the peaks and ridges looked. There are 42 other mountains between 29,000' and 19,000'. Mt. Everest, at 29,029', is the tallest.[4] Many of these mountains are sacred and unclimbed. It was thrilling to be so close to this entire region, which is held sacred by the Gurung people who live there. It was easy to understand why Nepalese believe that demons, genies, and gods live in the mountains. So do I. On a more recent trip, I asked our guide, as he was gazing at the mountains, if there were any legends about them. Although he spoke English, he didn't understand the question. This made sense, because I'd heard that mystics and psychics believe some information is too sacred to share.

Later, I learned that people living in the Himalayan mountains believe they are connected to the mountains and all of nature. For them, there isn't a mind-body split, and spirituality is not just a concept. Everything is connected to nature. The feeling of intense life, commingled with the mystical and magical, is confusing, profound, and seductive. People who see and feel this realm will never see things again the same way.[5]

---

[4] Ibid, Cheneviere, Introduction

[5] Ibid, Cheneviere, Introduction

Chapter 4—Our Daily Routine

Imagine a place where exact time becomes irrelevant. Each day followed the same rhythmic pattern and began about 6 a.m., when our cook's assistant with bright eyes and an impish smile brought sherpa tea and a bowl of warm water for washing our faces to our tent. After tea, the next step was to pack our duffel bags, put them outside the tent and go to the meal tent. Our duffel bags were lined with plastic garbage bags to protect our belongings from rain and dust. After a couple of frantic mornings trying to pack, we learned to compartmentalize our bags and pack quickly.

Most mornings were warm enough for us to eat breakfast outside while gazing at the scenery. Breakfast included variations of eggs, hot cereal, toast, and strong coffee. While we ate, our porters packed our tents and bags and left to reach our lunch spot. Each time we arrived for lunch or at our campsite, we were greeted with a smile and a refreshing glass of juice. We hiked about three hours in the morning, had a leisurely lunch over an hour to rest, and then hiked another three or four hours to camp. If there wasn't enough time for our cook to prepare a hot lunch, he prepared a lunch of salad, salami, and cheese. When we reached camp at the end of our day, our tents were already set up with our bags and our sleeping bags unrolled. We slept on an air mattress underneath two high-quality North Face bags, a light one inside a heavier one. After we had juice, we returned to our tents to rest and wash with another bowl of warm water. What a welcome relief to take our boots and hiking clothes off, stretch out on our sleeping bags, and change into cleaner clothes over the long underwear we slept in.

After a few days, we didn't care anymore about how our hair looked or how dirty we were. Since the air was pure, we didn't feel sticky and slimy. Baby wipes were enough to freshen up and use to wash. We washed our underwear and socks in the bowls of warm water and hung them to dry on the lines inside our tents. If our socks were still damp the next morning, we tied them to dry on the outside of our packs. After a short rest, it was time for tea, cookies, or popcorn served in the dining tent. I loved this time to chat about the day. Then we walked back to our tent to read and rest until dinner.

Our cook's bell rang after an hour or so, to let us know dinner was ready. Nepalese food is similar to Indian food with variations of curry, turmeric, cumin, coriander, garlic, fenugreek seed, mango powder, mustard oil, garlic, ginger, and other spices. Typically, ghee (a kind of clarified butter) isn't used as it is in Indian food. We ate fresh vegetables bought from farms along the way, beans, various types of lentils, greens, and meat. One night our cook made pizza, just like we enjoyed in the States, and another night he used a pressure cooker to bake a cake for us at a high altitude.

After dinner, snuggled happily in our sleeping bags, reading with our headlamps, my friend and I fell asleep while listening to our guides' happy conversation while they had dinner and worked. Sleep came among the sounds of crickets and countless other insects and an occasional barking dog. During the nights, I dragged myself out of my warm sleeping bag to relieve myself and was struck by the silence and the close sensation of brilliant stars, which enveloped me with inner peace and a deep connection to myself along with a deep connection to nature. It felt like I was in heaven.

Our daily hikes took us past small shrines to the Hindu gods, prayer flags and chortens, and sacred piles of stones along the trail made by Nepalese people. Rocks are placed into a pile to be walked reverently clockwise around while sending blessings to the world. To me there are few things more beautiful than the colorful prayer flags fluttering in the wind, sometimes waving gently, sometimes raging; often faded. Each color used in prayer flags represents a part of nature. The white represents air; the red, fire; the green, water; the yellow, earth; and the blue, space. It is believed good merit is created for our troubled world by putting prayer flags up for the benefit of other living beings. Ancient Buddhist prayers known as mantras, and the symbols displayed on the flags, produce a spiritual vibration that is carried by the wind across the countryside.

The most common mantra used by Nepalese is Tibetan. Tibetan Buddhists believe that saying the mantra "Om Mani Padme Hum" out loud or silently to oneself invokes the powerful benevolent attention and blessings of Chenrezig, the embodiment of compassion. Viewing the written form of the mantra is said to have the same effect. It is often carved into mani stones and on prayer flags. Silent prayers are considered to be blessings dissolved in the wind to extend to others. The belief is that all beings that are touched by the wind are uplifted and a little happier. It seemed like the prayer flags, the kind men and women carrying heavy loads of wood, fruit, and vegetables, the breath-taking scenery we saw along the way, and our stops at cheerful tea houses all helped us continue our trek.

The first time I approached one of Nepal's long, very high, suspension bridges over a deep valley or river, my stomach flipped. Sensing how I felt, one of the guides gently took my arm, and across we went! By the end of the trek, I easily crossed these bridges by myself while the guides clapped and cheered for me.

I was deeply touched by how happy, generous, and sincerely caring the hard-pressed Nepalese people were. Their joyful spirits melted my heart. On the trail, we were greeted again and again with a smile, both palms together placed at their hearts and saying, "Namaste." A Sanskrit word, Namaste means "I honor the place in you where the spirit lives. I honor the place in you which is of Love, of Truth, of Light, of Peace. When you are in that place in you, and I am in that place in me, then we are one."

During our trek, Kathy spoke many of the different village dialects in the villages, and knew some of the locals. She introduced us to a Nepalese woman who welcomed us into her tiny home for tea. We could barely fit to sit on the dirt floor and accept her hospitality. She smiled broadly at us and seemed genuinely interested and pleased to have us visit her while she served us hot sweet tea from small china cups.

The day before our last night of camping, Kathy explained that we'd have a celebration with the staff. She encouraged us to think of a way to thank them. My fun-loving friend suggested we do a shadow puppet show. During the day we collected sticks and found pieces of cardboard to make puppets. We asked our staff to sit outside the dining tent while we used light from our flashlights behind the puppets to make shadows on the tent wall. Our show was about the trek and some of the mishaps along the way.

They loved it. Having never seen a TV before, they wondered if they were seeing a TV or a movie. To thank us, they placed a white, silk ceremonial scarf, a khatak, around each of our necks, symbolizing purity and compassion and wishing us luck on our journey. These long silken scarves are used for births, weddings, funerals, and ceremonies. The Tibetan ones are usually white, symbolizing the pure heart of the giver, though it is quite common to find yellow or gold khataks as well.

By the time we got back to Kathmandu, I understood why most people who visit Nepal, like myself, don't want to leave. I felt more alive than I'd been for a very long time. I had been taken care of and supported by our staff for 21 days. Being close to nature, breathing clean air, eating organic food, trekking, and resting my mind for three weeks was wonderfully energizing and empowering. I left wanting to retain the level of fitness I had achieved and to continue feeling open and optimistic about my life. I continue to marvel at how this journey led me to the creation of an unimaginable accomplishment. It changed the trajectory of my life.

Before leaving Kathmandu, Kathy introduced me to her husband, Gary McCue, a tall, lanky, ex-hippy from Rochester, New York with a long, gray ponytail, who had lived in Kathmandu for nearly 20 years. Gary mentioned that he and Kathy were taking a group to Bhutan and hoped I'd join. I'd never thought of going to Bhutan, and couldn't imagine how it would be possible.

Chapter 5—Journeys Through Time: Bhutan, a Himalayan Kingdom, 2002

Two years before, the year of the new millennium, I returned home from trekking the Annapurna Circuit in Nepal to continue my day-to-day routine as a clinical social worker for Montgomery County, Maryland, and long hours working in private practice. As a single parent, I struggled to balance work and caring for my son and daughter, our two large dogs, and our beloved cat. I felt different after that first trek, more aware of still being bogged down in life's minutiae and worrying needlessly about things I couldn't change, but I was seeing through new eyes. My life was lighter, infused with the lessons Nepal had taught me. Over and above all, I was more resilient and open to finding joy and acceptance no matter the circumstances. I'd learned what was important. In short, I was stronger than I thought and knew I was on a spiritual journey. The magical mountains seemed to draw me back to re-experience the freedom, peace, exhilaration, and wonder that I had felt there.

In this state of mind, I recalled the invitation from our guide, Kathy, and her husband, Gary, two years earlier in Kathmandu, to join them to trek in Bhutan. Gary's book, *Trekking in Tibet: A Traveler's Guide*, had become a second bible for those on Himalayan expeditions. His "laid-back trekking (LBT) approach" was based on the idea that the slower you go (as long as you don't come into camp in the dark!) and the closer to the back of the trek group you are, the more often amazing things tend to happen. You can race along the trails anywhere in the world with a view of the toes of your boots; but by slowing down, you can take in the incredible surroundings and truly experience what attracted you to a region in the first place. After trekking with Gary and Kathy, I grew to appreciate their nuanced cultural understanding, which opened unique doors for us. They spoke many different dialects of the Nepalese and Tibetan languages and had lived in Nepal for over 25 years. Their laughter and easy-going natures helped us shrug off some of our trip's unavoidable snags.

Less than one year after 9/11, and in the midst of the 2002 Beltway Sniper shootings in Maryland, Virginia, and Washington, D.C. that killed 10 people and terrified everyone, I registered for the trip to Bhutan that would take me to the northernmost part of the Himalayans, close to India. I felt a sense of mystery and intrigue just thinking about the journey.

Only two years after my introduction to trekking in Annapurna, Kathy and Gary would guide me for three weeks in what is known as the "The Land of the

Thunder Dragon"—isolated, remote, and exotic. The Thunder Dragon of Bhutanese mythology has been the national symbol of Bhutan for centuries, long before the establishment of its government in 1907. The Bhutanese cherish their unique cultural heritage and, to discourage its alteration (particularly by Western values), tourism is strictly regulated and limited. It is renowned for being a country that measures its GDP in terms of happiness rather than economic output.

Marilyn Mason, a consultant/social worker living in New Mexico, coordinated and organized our group of five stateside. It consisted of a father-daughter team—Julia, who traveled from Tibet where she was studying the grasslands, and her successful businessman father from Philadelphia; also Phyllis, a yoga teacher working at Canyon Ranch, Arizona; Mitchell, from Maine, who didn't seem to need to work; and me. The trip was described as "Journeys through Time: Bhutan, a Himalayan Kingdom." In our itinerary, Marilyn described Bhutan as: "One of the most exclusive and rare destinations in the world, lying just south of Tibet, east of Nepal and Sikkim. Mystery surrounds Bhutan's distant past, dating back to the eighth century. With pristine rivers, towering crags, green hills, and magnificent snow-peaked mountains, land-locked Bhutan is filled with Buddhist myths and legends."

Who could resist that? Certainly not me. Before we left, Marilyn suggested we take turns writing a group journal while we were on the journey.

Our group met in the Bangkok airport at 5:30 a.m., allowing us to travel on a one-group visa to Bhutan. The flight into Paro's single-runway airport was an exciting approach, wending through steep-sided valleys and landing safely to the applause of the passengers. I didn't know about the approach beforehand, and so looking out the window with the plane threading its way through the mountains, I stopped breathing. It was no wonder the tiny airport, nestled among sharp peaks of up to 18,000 feet, is said to be one of the most dangerous airports in the world. It is 1.5 miles above sea level, and only select pilots are qualified to land there.

We embarked in 7,656 feet high Thimphu, the capital, a one-street town of red, green, and yellow-painted storefronts. Some had only a ladder to enter. Before we climbed one of them to a restaurant for lunch, we mingled with the 2,000 Buddhist practitioners gathered for spiritual teachings nearby in a field the size of a football stadium. Brightly colored awnings, archways and temples surrounded the covered seating area. It was like looking at a movie set. Tamdin, our Sidar (lead guide), born and raised in Thimphu, offered details about the local architecture, which adheres to laws that require structures be built in the Bhutanese traditional design: three stories high, using mostly stone, rammed earth, local timber and bamboo. Animals, traditionally housed on the ground floor, are now outlawed for health reasons so that space is used for storage. On the second floor, grain and household items are stored, and the third floor is for housing. I was taken aback by the clay sculptures of large red penises hanging from the eaves of many homes, until I learned they were used to promote fertility. Tandin explained about the custom of chewing betel nuts, which grow on plants throughout the region. They are small red nuts with narcotic properties. Their red color stains the teeth and lips. Most people we saw had red-stained mouths.

The few days we spent sightseeing and hiking gave our bodies time to become acclimated to the altitude. It also gave us access to places less adventurous travelers never see, and to learn about Bhutan"s customs, national dress code, monastic practices, music, and dance. In Buddhist traditions, Rinpoches are the most revered and educated people in the region. Their education is the equivalent of multiple PhDs in the United States.

Tandin, the next Rinpoche's nephew, was able to take us into monasteries built in the fifteenth century, usually closed to tourists. After he spoke with the watchman who was guarding the monasteries and offered him betel nuts, the man would unlock the door and allow us to enter the sacred temples. Each time through the ornately carved wooden doors, I felt as if I was walking into another realm, one that echoed centuries of chanting, studying, and esoteric Buddhist rituals. The natural light, incense, art, and burning candles enveloped and filled me with peace.

The last day before we began our trek, we journeyed to the Cheri (iron) monastery. It began with a 45-minute drive, then we walked for an hour, under a piercing blue sky and puffy white clouds through a covered bridge across the river, until we reached the monastery. The air, water, and trees seemed to shimmer in the sunlight. A goral (a cross between an antelope and a goat), a white horse, and a couple of friendly dogs peacefully waited on the monastery grounds. Before we entered the hallowed space, Gary told us that in the 17th century, Shabdrung Nawang (1594-1651) was forced to flee from Tibet, although he was enthroned as the 18th Abbot of Ralung, the seat of the hereditary lineage and the first monastery to be established in Tibet. In Bhutan after his escape, he built the monastery when he was 19 years old, and he was credited with unifying Bhutan. Tamdin explained that when these exalted beings die (those believed to be reincarnations of enlightened rinpoches), their bodies are kept from decomposing by being painted with gold and positioned in a lotus pose in secret rooms in monasteries. Only the highest monks are permitted to see their teacher's dead bodies after they die. Several times a day, food and other offerings are left for the deceased.

The guardian unlocked the doors for us. After we took off our boots and entered the temple, our eyes adjusted and through the dim light, we saw an enormous gold Buddha with soft eyes and a welcoming gesture. The Buddha was flanked by fierce statues of animal protectors at his feet. Their bulging eyes and barred fangs were meant to protect him. The air was thick and pungent from incense. Ancient scriptures were stored along the walls in wooden bookcases inlayed in blue, red, and yellow designs carved by devoted monks. The walls were covered with frescos depicting the cycle of life, illustrating the origin and cause of human suffering and the path to liberation. Gary whispered to us that the earth-colored chortens are important, because they contain Buddha's sacred artifacts and teachings. A chorten consists of a square foundation symbolizing the earth, a dome symbolizing water, and thirteen tapering steps to enlightenment symbolizing the element of fire.

While I stood gazing and absorbing the artistry and atmosphere, I slipped into a dream-like state and felt slightly dizzy and nauseated. It seemed that I was in the presence of the power of the universes. I savored the time, knowing this was a rare opportunity handed to me. My entire being felt expanded, awed, and peaceful. It seemed as if time had stopped. When it was time to leave, we were permitted to light a candle, and each of us left small monetary offerings on the altar beneath the Buddha's feet. I wished I could have stayed longer to carry inside me the euphoria of that experience.

The next day, we eagerly started our trek on a trail along the Paro Chhu River. Before we started our trek, Marilyn reminded us about our shared journal, each of us writing a page a day. Kathy described our journey that day.

In our journal, Kathy wrote, "The river was our constant companion, raging and roaring and preventing conversation. At other times, the Paro was calm and translucent, reflecting sunlight. Sometimes the mud grabbed our boots, not wanting to let go. Other times, the mud provided a soft path, very gentle on the knees, which took us through a few villages into the most 'alive' forest I had ever seen. Moss, lichen, ferns, and flowers grew from the trunks of trees and branches. It seemed enchanted. Twisted limbs dripped epiphytes and sunlight filtered through wispy lichen. It seemed as though we might see fairies or hairy goblins at any moment. I wondered if leopards or even tigers were watching us. There were countless shades of green and as many sizes of leaves."

After our first two days of trekking, in which we averaged six hours daily and ascended 4,000 feet,

Marilyn decided to return to Thimpu because she realized she wasn't in shape to continue the demanding trail. She rode back to town on one of the ponies led by Tamdin. We sadly watched them leave. The rest of us continued to trek past steep slopes where yaks and blue sheep found only in the Himalayas grazed, and stunning mountain lakes. The stress and anxiety we carried with us from our lives at home fell away. When we walked through villages, Gary and Kathy introduced us to families they knew from previous trips so we could experience their kindness and see how they lived. We were welcomed into their homes for tea. Most of them had never seen a camera before and were amazed at photos of themselves for the first time. After I got home, I sent photos to the people we photographed via the travel company, but I don't know if they ever got them. From time to time, at certain spots, we came upon Indian guards standing near the trail, presumably to intercept forbidden smugglers and to protect the borders.

In addition to this ethereal mountain backdrop, we saw huge forests, blue poppies, orchids, and countless birds as we slowly made our way. Much like the terrain, the weather could change dramatically. Sometimes we wore T-shirts in the sunlight, sometimes our heavy jackets through fog and wind. Our days were simplified into hiking, eating, and sleeping. Along the way, different issues came up for each of us, like feeling tired, frustrated, or scared. For the sake of *esprit de corps*, we kept them to ourselves, except Phyllis. One day, shaken and anxious, she asked Gary, "Where is the path?" He answered, "There isn't one." She was overwhelmed by the emptiness of the wide-open space, and agreed to ride a pony led by a young man working with us.

The day before we crossed Botey La Pass (at 16,135 feet), our cook prepared lunch for us in a ruined fortress which was once an important defensive outpost for Bhutan against invasions from Tibet. The night before we crossed the pass, we camped in a valley surrounded by mountains and a clear sky. At dawn, after the snowfall, I went to Mitchell's tent to urge him to come out and look at the shimmering, otherworldly sight. "Mitchell, you've got to see this! It's incredible!" He came out of his tent to take photographs, and later he confessed, "I was frightened when it snowed. I was terrified that we'd be snowed in." That thought had never crossed my mind. I was completely exhilarated and realized I trusted that things would work out, in spite of the inevitable obstacles and challenges we encountered on our journey.

After breakfast, the group started our slow ascent, spread out as we labored up the steep trail on stiff heavy legs to the pass, slowly in the thin air with frequent stops to rest. It was a test of endurance.

If I'd thought much about this trip beforehand, I probably never would have registered for it; but there I was, taking one step at a time. Gradually, all logical thought dissolved. In good spirits, Gary walked effortlessly on his long legs back and forth along the trail, encouraging us and giving us chocolate that he said was the same kind Sir Edmund Hillary with Tensing Norgay and his crew used to climb Everest, the tallest mountain in the world at 29,029 feet. After several hours of steady, slow walking, sitting occasionally to gaze out over the valley, watching the snow pigeons flying over the canyons below us, and listening to the wind, I reached the pass just after Mitchell. The view was exalting and terrifying, accompanied by stillness and producing a sense that I could see clearly into myself and the infinite unknowable.

We stood together under tattered, faded, wind-whipped red, white, blue, and green prayer flags, contemplating the mountains and valleys falling steeply away from the pass on each side. I said, "I don't think I could trek any higher than this, do you?" Mitchell answered ruminatively, "It depends on where you are going, don't you think?" His answer made me pause and wonder where life might take me after this pilgrimage.

Reluctantly, we started down the precipitous sloping path, the 15 horses and mules carrying our tents and gear plodding in front of us. I felt exhilarated, buoyant, and filled with the certainty that I could accomplish more than I had thought possible. My future started opening up in ways I could only have dreamed of before this adventure.

On our last night in camp, our cook made a celebratory dinner for us, and the staff built a large campfire that was conducive to lively conversation about personal stories and tips for our staff, followed by dancing around the fire. The men who'd cared for us during the trek danced their native dances and we joined them reverently.

As we walked back to town the next day, we looked forward to one of the best parts of such demanding treks—the simple pleasure of a shower or bath and changing into clean clothes upon returning to a lodge. Julia (of the father-daughter team) and I decided to immerse ourselves in a traditional Bhutanese Menchu. These cleansing treatments for the body have a medical component to them. Heated river rocks are placed in water where they crack and steam, releasing minerals and relieving deep-seated aches. Widely practiced in Bhutan, this practice is considered a curative treatment for various aches and illnesses. Before the actual bathing, firewood, and stones are gathered from the nearby forest, piled together, and burned until the stones are red hot. Various herbs, like mugwort, wormwood, or sagebrush, known for their powerful homeopathic Ayurvedic healing properties, are combined into an often closely held family formula and are added to heated spring water, along with some aromatic Artemisia leaves, whose essential oils further enhance the healing properties. Julia and I luxuriated in outdoor wooden tubs prepared for us inside a wooden hut, similar to a sauna in the United States, but more rustic and free from artificial lights, music and buzz.

As I lounged in the tub, buoyant in the water, it gradually sank in that this healing applied to far more than our climb on that unforgettable day. This trek was transformative for me. I felt more connected to my authentic self, desires, and passions. How did I choose my direction and goals? How resolute was I to push past my imagined limitations like not having enough time, income, or skills? Where was I going? I had a sense of never turning back. I'll never forget the thrill of making it to that pass, and the gratitude I felt standing under the forever-fluttering prayer flags. Afterward, Julia and I wrapped ourselves in blankets and stretched out on the nearby stones until we were ready to return to our hotel for dinner. I felt euphoric, free of life burdens and worries, and hungry to do another trek somewhere else in the Himalayan Mountains.

After three wonder-filled weeks in Bhutan, I returned to my American life, filled with optimism and open to possibilities. On one of my first days back at work, a colleague called to tell me about a life coach training program. She was taking it and suggested I would like it too. "There are no coincidences." I thought this was an opportunity in-waiting. I wanted to know more, and when I called to inquire, I learned that, unlike other programs, this one was taught "from the inside out" and guided clients to discover their core values. When I called to inquire, I learned Life Coaching is based on Solution Oriented Therapy and Positive Psychology. The trainers taught skills and helped people discover what they are passionate about, write a plan to reach their goals, and execute the plan. The two founders happened to be my teachers and coaches, a bonus. I jumped into their program. Enrolling meant somehow managing to cram work, classes, and meetings into my already crowded schedule. I wondered whether I could commit and follow through on such a demanding goal. Then I remembered standing under the forever fluttering, tattered, red, white, blue and yellow prayer flags on the heights of Botey La Pass. I suddenly knew deep in my heart where I was going.

My training group listened intently as I described the challenges and joy of my trekking expeditions. They helped me to flesh out the idea of trekking as a metaphor that describes the ups and downs, unexpected events, beauty, joy, and hard work of making life changes. I found a way to share this with other seekers. I married my counseling skills with my passion for trekking. My intention was to help guide others in a physical, as well as psychological, journey toward gaining self-knowledge and to bring courage and fulfillment to their lives. The seeds that had been planted after my first trek two years before began to unfurl their tender leaves toward the sun. A few days later, a copy of our Bhutan journal arrived in the mail, which returned me to our experience.

As a student in the nine-month program, I was coached and did all the exercises involved in creating a life plan for myself based on my values. In order to become certified with the International Federation of Life Coaches, I took several more training programs and a final exam during the next three years to become a Certified Life Coach.

Chapter 6—Everest Adventure, Nepal 2004

In the midst of the training program, a catalog arrived from Wilderness Travel. I opened it eagerly to see which trips would take me back to Nepal. An 18-day trip to the Everest Mountain region appealed to me. By this time, I'd learned that if I set my intention to go on a trip like this, everything would fall into place, giving me enough time and money to go. No one had anticipated the 9/11 tragedy in 2001 or the SARS epidemic. Most United States citizens were afraid to travel so soon after this horrific event. Like everyone else in our group, I was nervous about traveling but didn't let that stop me.

In hindsight, this trip to Nepal was a turning point in my journey. When I landed in Kathmandu, I had little knowledge about the political unrest disrupting Nepal at the time. The Maoists were demonstrating for more equality and there were young soldiers holding rifles standing on each corner. One of the shopkeepers I visited gently suggested I tell people I was from Canada; it would be safer for me.

Our group consisted of eight men and women. Two couples from New Mexico, a couple from

Massachusetts, and another single woman, who requested a single room, and me. Our leader was Steve Webster, a tall slender British man who lived with his two daughters and his Nepalese wife, Neeru, in Kathmandu. He'd been in the travel business for over 20 years and had a talent for facilitating groups.

After spending a couple of nights in Kathmandu, we flew on a tiny plane to a mountainside airstrip at Lukla (9,200'), the starting point for climbers to reach Mount Everest Base Camp. Although the flying distance is short, rain commonly occurs in Lukla while the sun is shining brightly in Kathmandu. High winds, cloud cover and changing visibility often delayed flights or closed the airport. Our flight was uneventful except for the spectacular flight in-between mountains that looked like snow-covered palaces.

When we landed, Lukla was electric with excitement. Busy Sherpas (the ethnic group in that region) gathered supplies, their crew and climbers. Our sherpa and staff were there waiting for us. We enjoyed tea while our crew packed our duffel bags and supplies. The trek started by ascending through a number of villages, crossing suspension bridges over raging rivers built alongside primitive fragile bridges that people used to cross carrying heavy loads. Originally, they were built by Sir Edmund Hillary's Himalayan Trust. In contrast to the

Annapurna region, the Everest region seemed stark and barren.

After a long steep climb, we entered Sagarmatha (Mt. Everest) National Park before the ascent of Namche Hill. Gradually we ascended a steep forested hillside on switchback trails leading to Namche Bazaar (11,270'), a bustling village well-known to trekkers and climbers. We stayed in our sherpa's bright comfortable lodge instead of camping the first night.

From Namche, we had panoramic views of Thamserku and Kwangde directly across the Bhote Kosi Valley from the ridge above town. We could see Everest and many of the other giant peaks of the Khumbu. Before dawn the next morning, we went to a ridge to see the sun rise over these majestic mountains, which inspired us with their sheer beauty and majesty.

Before we left town, we visited the colorful weekly outdoor market on the south side, where Tibetan traders with red bands around their heads sold merchandise like batteries, shoes, clothes, crafts, colorful blankets, water buffalo, yaks and horses herded up from the foothills by Rai traders. Many had crossed the 19,050' high Nangpa La, the traditional Sherpa trading route from Tibet. Sadly, the pass is closed now since China annexed Tibet.

After we left Namche, we walked through a lush, forested area, past many walls of mani stones

(stones carved with mantras), through a rhododendron forest to the beautiful ridge top site of Tengboche Monastery, surrounded by the Kangtega ("Snow Saddle," 22,235'), Thamserku ("Three Goddesses," 21,674') and Ama Dablam ("Mother's Charm Box," 22,494') mountains, several of the most spectacular peaks in the Himalayas. Our porters set up camp for us in a small field near the monastery facing these majestic mountains.

While we were there, we were invited by a monk to meet Rinpoche Tenzin Jangpo. At the time I knew this was a rare opportunity, considering current world politics and previous experiences with my spiritual teacher, but I didn't know how significant it would prove to be. At the agreed-upon time, we entered the dark monastery through a room decorated with ancient bright blue and red tapestries, carpets, small statues of buddhas, and the smell of incense burning. It was a deeply moving experience to be in the presence of such a revered teacher.

We sat respectfully on benches along the walls while he spoke with us with the help of his translator. He told us that most of the high rinpoches from the surrounding countries planned to meet in Kathmandu to discuss the events of 9/11 and how to contribute to world peace. After he spoke, we were given permission to ask a question. When it was my turn, I asked, "What can we do to help create world peace?" He suggested that we could take something, perhaps a small Buddha, back to the United States to remind us of the kindness and peace we experienced in Nepal. I didn't really understand what he meant, but contemplated his answer and then forgot it until years later.

After we returned to Kathmandu, Steve took us to visit the young residents of the Himalayan Foundation School. Children came from remote villages and lived there to be educated. Following our visit, we had lunch in Steve's small lodge, Shivapuri Heights Cottage, which he and his wife built in the foothills above Kathmandu. We were charmed by the location and the attention to design and detail, and wished we could stay.

PART II—MY BUSINESS IDEA GETS OFF THE GROUND

Chapter 7—The Name of My Business

Once again, I returned to my American life filled with optimism and open to new opportunities. When the catalog arrived for the conference I attend every year in Washington, D.C., I noticed the co-founder of the Institute for Life Coaching, Pat Williams—my teacher—was giving a workshop. We agreed to meet in person for breakfast at the conference. After a brief conversation, he invited me to join his advisory board for his project, titled Coaching the Global Village, which he hoped would take coaching to developing countries. I accepted his invitation. This board worked together for the next two years to develop a training program to teach participants three levels of listening, how to ask powerful questions, and how to hold others accountable. I loved working with other like-minded people, and formed a lasting friendship with Rich Tafel, another group member who lived in Washington, D.C.

One night, after providing successful training to childcare workers in Montgomery County, we went out to dinner to celebrate our achievement. We were encouraged and excited about how well the training had gone. I wondered why Rich wasn't there and called him. He was turned around and appreciated that I called and stood in front of the restaurant until he arrived. Later, he told me that I was the only one who knew how to pull a group together and move the project forward. I was astounded by his feedback because I had never thought of myself that way.

When the conversation turned to me and my coaching business, Pat wrote some ideas on a napkin and suggested a name for my coaching program. It was The Trek of Life. We talked about how life is like a trek. It is a long journey with ups and downs, unexpected obstacles, and highlights, which usually require help from others along the way.

I loved coaching and hoped I'd get clients by word of mouth as I did in my private practice, but this didn't happen. Over dinner one night, Rich told me about a marketing program he was taking and urged me to enroll. I was skeptical and bitter and didn't want to spend more time and money unless the program could really deliver. But I called the trainers, Michael Charest and Eileen Redden, who would be my coaches. They impressed me. In my first coaching session with Eileen, I burst into tears on the call after she gave me authentic support and encouragement for my ideas for The Trek of Life, and suggested I change the name to The Trek of Your Life. The year-long training program was interesting and required 8-10 hours of work each week. Again, I used my annual leave to attend weekly ninety-minute classes and coaching sessions. On weekends, I did homework and learned to create marketing strategies for my coaching program.

One of the recommended strategies was public speaking. Like most people, I hated public speaking and actually froze when I had to speak in front of groups. I avoided it at all costs. When Michael offered a 3-day training in speaking, I took the opportunity. I understood that speaking was a valuable tool and had no idea how to do it. Most of the other people in the training had experience giving presentations. I was intimidated and fumbled my presentation. Nevertheless, the training was helpful. One of the other participants suggested that I join a Toastmasters group. I joined one as soon as I returned to Maryland. By participating in a club, I overcame my fear of speaking to groups of people and learned specific presentation skills. Our club President encouraged me to write this book! I never would have even thought of writing a book without his encouragement.

Chapter 8—Sacred Mountains and Hidden Monasteries: Tibet 2009 and an Idea

In 2009, Wilderness Travel sent a notice that Kathy Butler was going to lead a trip to Eastern Tibet titled, "The Heart of Kham, Sacred Mountains and Hidden Monasteries of Eastern Tibet." Without much thought, I registered for the trip and later learned this trip was more of a cultural trip with hours of driving, some hiking, and camping. By this time, my children and my boss were used to me doing things like this, and my annual leave was approved without much questioning.

Tibet fascinated me, and I was eager to trek with Kathy again. A week before I left, a Wilderness Travel staff member called to explain that Kathy couldn't lead the trip because her father had died. She explained that Gary would leave a group he was leading in Nepal early, cross the mountains with our staff, and meet us somewhere along the way.

Our sherpa met our group of seven in Chengdu, China to ascend to the Tibetan plateau. My roommate was from D.C., and we'd met before the trip once we learned we'd be sharing a room. There were two couples and a reporter from *The New York Times*, who was returning to New York after working in Afghanistan. After a couple of days sightseeing in

Chengdu, we drove hours past three of Asia's greatest rivers, the Yangtze, Mekong, and Salween, which forge tremendous gorges through Kham. Somehow, Gary found us after a few days. He arrived with a terrible cold, but in good spirits considering his arduous trip over the mountains from Kathmandu. I was happy to see him again.

We traveled on newly built roads, which were often blocked by landslides. Many times, we waited hours for the road to be cleared. Sometimes Gary or our cook found a tea shop owner who would rent the kitchen, allowing our staff to offer tea, coffee, and snacks for us to enjoy while we waited. Sometimes it took hours. I used any occasion like these, or when the drivers stopped, to take a break to walk along the road until the drivers caught up to me. We rarely saw other tourists and were frequently stopped by stern Chinese police for visas and passport checks.

We traveled by icy glaciers tumbling down from jagged peaks, through lush spruce forests, grand monasteries, and temples, which were scattered along old caravan routes following the rivers where much of the agriculture is located. Colorful prayer flags flapped everywhere, enlivening the landscape. The lower altitude in much of this region supported larger herds of yak, sheep, goats, and horses. The ancient Tibetan Buddhist religion in this region was vibrant due to fewer political constraints.

Our nights in the hotels were grim. Often the light didn't work, and if there was water, it was ice cold. Members of our group were apprehensive about camping since they'd never done it. They didn't believe me when I told them they'd love it, and it was more comfortable than the hotels we visited. Once we started to camp, they understood and loved the experience. Our campsites were in fields near monasteries, surrounded by vast grasslands or by lush forests and pristine streams. We were always surrounded by nature, even though we were camped near a road. Often, we camped in fields near herders who brought their yak herds to the plains in the summer. The campsites in fields near the monasteries felt peaceful and serene. In a couple of the monasteries, we saw artists from Lhasa sitting on scaffolds, quietly painting the walls near the magnificent Buddha statues with fierce, open-mouthed statues of lion-like protectors near their feet. We learned that if the Tibetans knew Chinese officials were coming, they'd hide all the photos of the Dalai Lama and the money for donations. Luckily, that never happened while we were there—though when we arrived in Litang for the horse festival, it was canceled because the Chinese government didn't want foreigners visiting the region. We were really disappointed. Nevertheless, I loved seeing the horsemen riding across the vast plains. One of my fondest memories was seeing young girls, about ten years old, wearing leggings, brown dresses, and unkempt hair, on the plains herding hundreds of yaks with dogs, their piercing whistles and rocks from their slingshots.

Often, young and old Tibetans visited us just because they were curious, and because we looked so foreign to them. One evening, we were invited to visit a family in their yurt. Motorcycles were parked in front instead of ponies. When we entered, we were invited to sit on the floor and have yak butter tea. It was an honor to join them, but the tea tasted terrible to me. I pretended to sip it and hoped I wasn't offending the family. In one area there was a portrait of the Dalai Lama, indicating their devotion. In other parts there was a burning fire, pots for cooking, and piled-up bed rolls. There were a couple of young children, their parents, and elderly people all living there together.

One day while I was hiking with Gary, an idea came to me. I wondered about creating a voluntourism business bringing groups to the Himalayas. When I asked Gary, which country I should choose, he responded instantly, "Nepal, it is so cuddly for tourists." I knew what he meant.

Chapter 9—Voluntourism Trips to Nepal

After I returned from Tibet, I emailed Steve in Nepal asking if he'd be interested in creating a voluntourism trip together. He responded enthusiastically. "Yes, you get the group together, and I'll handle everything on the ground in Nepal."

I asked myself, "How in the world am I going to do this?" Talk to Rich, of course. Occasionally, we got together to have pizza and talked about coaching, social justice projects, and spirituality. When I asked him what he thought of my idea, he suggested we trade coaching sessions. I jumped at the opportunity. Rich helped me create the concepts for The Trek of Your Life and continued to advise me. The goal of my business was to add meaning and purpose to baby boomers' and Generation Xers' lives by engaging them in global causes larger than themselves. Baby boomers are the healthiest, wealthiest, best-educated generation the planet will ever have. Most retire around 60 years old and have 20 more years to live and contribute. Most yearn to do something purposeful—if not, they leave 20 years on the table. Since COVID, more and more young people are yearning for more balanced purposeful lives.

TOYL offered service-oriented group tours to Nepal, where participants would engage in their own inner and outer journeys while serving others. To start the business, I devoted my weekends to creating a website and flyers and writing speeches to market my program.

Meanwhile, because of budget cuts, there were more regulations and personnel changes where I worked; I was increasingly stressed and struggled with making the decision to retire. Like others who make the decision to leave their secure job, I was terrified. Eventually, after hours and weeks of listening to me agonize about my decision, Rich said, "Sydney, you will never get your business off the ground unless you quit." He was right; I needed to walk my talk and gather my courage to leave my job after nearly 23 years.

In addition to the financial planning involved, I knew it was important for me to be part of another professional community, and I rejoined the Greater Washington Society of Clinical Social Workers. When I attended their annual potluck supper, I approached the President and offered to volunteer on the hospitality committee, or something like it.

Chapter 10—Wilderness Travel: Exploratory Journey to Lo Manthang and Beyond, May 2010, or Mustang, the Last Kingdom in Nepal

A few months before I submitted my resignation letter, I received a flyer from Wilderness Travel advertising an exploratory trek to Mustang, a journey to Lo Manthang and beyond. At about the same time, Gary sent me an email about this exploratory trip he was leading in Mustang, the last kingdom in Nepal on the border of Tibet. I'd read about Mustang in the Wilderness Travel catalog and wondered if I'd ever be able to go there.   The itinerary included descriptions of using ropes to climb into caves and 18,400-foot passes. I didn't think I could do it physically. Gary assured me in an email that I could; he explained the rope parts were optional. It was tempting to take this month-long trip and give notice to my boss that I'd be retiring when I returned.

After paying my deposit and making my airline reservations, I requested a month's annual leave. My boss declined my request. I was livid; I hated my job by this point and felt like quitting if she didn't approve my leave. The budget cuts were so deep that there weren't paper towels and toilet paper in the bathrooms. We cleaned our own offices and the waiting room. The grass around the building was knee-high. It was a demoralizing place for our clients and for the employees. I asked for a meeting with my boss, who reluctantly approved my leave when she learned I'd already made my flight reservations, and because she didn't want to lose another staff member.

Before leaving for Nepal, I attended an informal get-together to talk about getting more involved with the Greater Washington Society of Social Work. A couple of weeks later, Susan Post, who'd been the president for three years, called to ask if I'd like to be the next president. I was stunned and asked for more time to think about it. Later, when I casually talked this over with Rich, he said, "Go ahead, be president. It is fun to be president, and it'll look good on your resume." I decided to accept the nomination to be president, even though I didn't know any of the other officers or much about the organization. The executive committee understood that I wouldn't be fully on board until after making the trek and leaving my job.

Mustang is known as Little Tibet within Nepal.[6] But this itinerary describing the terrain, the caves,

---

[6]David Oliver Relin, *Second Suns*, 2013, page 160

and using ropes to climb, intimidated me. Still, the idea of taking a month-long trip before picking my "retirement" date was tempting. Gary, who was leading the trek, assured me I could not only physically handle it, but would enjoy it as well. Mustang, in north-central Nepal, is one of the nation's least developed and most inaccessible areas and had been restricted because of conflict with the Chinese along its border. *National Geographic* had recently done a film about their first expedition there. I was enchanted.

A week before I left, a Wilderness Travel staff person called to tell me I'd have a roommate, Pauline Green. We met for the first time in the lobby of Hotel Shangri-La in Kathmandu, and we hit it off immediately. Our time together sharing rooms, and a tent, and trekking together for the entire trip led to a long friendship. I learned later she had climbed Denali, Aconcagua, Kilimanjaro, a first ascent next to K-2, among others, and trekked in Peru, Nepal, Patagonia, the Arctic, Chile, Tibet, Pakistan, China, and Siberia. I had never even heard of many of these places. We've been friends ever since, and she continues to be genuinely interested in the nitty-gritty details of my work in Nepal. Her ideas, encouragement, and enthusiasm helped me through some doubtful, discouraging times related to getting this business off the ground. Imagine trying to find people willing to travel to a remote part of the world with someone they hardly knew. Pauline and her companion, Mo, joined the trek I led after the earthquake in Nepal in 2015.

Once I met our group, despite what Gary predicted, I felt way over my head. Our group consisted of 11--five who had single tents, four were Gary Groupies who continually took his trips and adored him, and two men who shared a double tent. One was an emergency room doctor turned chicken farmer with 13 chickens. He was accompanied by a man who climbed, kept fit by rowing, and had run in Death Valley.[7] To his credit, the doctor had been on Denali, Aconcagua, Vinson, Mallory's search on Everest and other big mountains, in spite of his 275 pounds. Both were Republicans who thought global warming was a government hoax.

Our trip began in May, in pre-monsoon weather. Since we'd all been to Kathmandu before, we drove South to the Newari town of Pharping, known for its Buddhist pilgrimage sites, to visit the Nyingma/Kargytip gompa with its statues, thangkas, and wall frescoes. We climbed the hillside draped in prayer flags to see a cave where the 8th Century Indian tantric master Guru Rinpoche (Padmasambhava) meditated. We left this peaceful, serene Buddhist site to visit Dakshinkali, a favorite

---

[7] Green, Pauline, Two Tablespoons of Sugar, Mustang, Nepal, p.1

Hindu pilgrimage destination, set at the confluence of two sacred streams in a rocky cleft in the forest, with a temple dedicated to the goddess Kali, the goddess of protection and fearlessness. Her statue shows her tongue sticking out to swallow evil and negative thoughts. Kali means "She who is black." She is generally depicted half-naked, with a garland of skulls, a belt of severed limbs, waving scary-looking weapons with two of her ten hands.[8]

To honor her, pilgrims take chickens, ducks, goats, sheep, pigs, and even the occasional buffalo up the path to be killed by skilled butchers who are also priests. Once the sacrifice is made, the meat goes into a pot nearby in the forest, where the pilgrims bring all the ingredients for a barbecue and spend the rest of the day feasting in the shade of the trees.[9] We visited Saturday, one of the big sacrificial days, to observe this sacrificial event which has profound spiritual significance for local people.[10] The approach to the temple from the bus stands wound through a religious bazaar, which is often hazy with smoke from barbecue fires. One of our group members bought a handsome red chicken from a

[8] http://www.religionfacts.com/hinduism/deities/goddesses.htm

[9] http://www.lonelyplanet.com/nepal/around-the-kathmandu-valley/dakshinkali

[10] Lonely planethttp://www.lonelyplanet.com/nepal/around-the-kathmandu-valley/dakshinkali

local farmer who sold produce for the ritual and was completely at ease carrying it up the path to be sacrificed. For our donation, the rest of us bought marigolds, coconuts, and powdered paint. Since only Hindus can enter the temple courtyard, we observed the ritual standing quietly on terraces near the temple where Kali resides. During the annual celebrations of Dashain in October, the temple is washed in blood and the image of Kali is bathed in gore from the sacrifices.

After a couple of days sightseeing in Kathmandu, we flew to Pokhara and spent the night in another Hotel Shangri-La with infinity pools and meticulously maintained British-inspired gardens. Pauline and I were the only ones who swam in the pool under a later afternoon blue sky. It was heavenly. Every evening, enormous brass bowls in the garden and hotel were filled with floating rose petals and candles.

Early the next morning we flew north, a short hop to Jomsom, a settlement of Tibetan-speaking people and district headquarters for the Annapurna region. When we arrived for our flight, Gary realized he'd left our tickets at the hotel! After a hectic scramble, we boarded our plane. In those days, the only way to get to Jomsom was to fly, trek or ride a pony, because there were no roads at that time. Our small plane took us through the Kali Gandaki River chasm, renowned as one of the world's deepest gorges, situated between Annapurna 1 (26,545') and Dhaulagiri (26,795'). The change from the lush environs of Pokhara to the dry desert landscape in the rain shadow of the Himalayas was dramatic.

We were greeted enthusiastically by our staff when we landed. They walked with us to our hotel in Thini, a short way from the landing strip. Our cook and sherpas quickly settled us into our stark rooms. We slept on the beds in our sleeping bags (in case there were bedbugs) and used the trickle of tepid water for a shower. To say we were in a remote area was an understatement.

The Tibetan Plateau is typically arid, because this region is in the rain shadow of the Annapurna Range. It was once the ocean floor, which accounts for the coral and ammonites we saw on our trek. Over 200 million years ago, the Indian continental plate crushed under Tibet, draining it and uplifting the whole Himalayan area. In fact, Mt. Everest is still rising a couple of feet every hundred years. This former seabed, an alluvial sea bottom, makes up the Tibetan Plateau. Rivers, rather than glaciers, cut into the plateaus leaving steep ravines. The endless winds sandblast the terrain, carving out Bryce Canyon-like hoodoos, or columns of sandstone.[11] There are caves in the canyon walls filled with

---

[11]., Pauline Green, Two Tablespoons of Sugar, p.7

fascinating Buddhist murals, artifacts, documents, and cave paintings, from 200-300 A.D.

After breakfast, our group hiked to explore the valley at 8,900 feet, a stark contrast to the arid plateau. We passed fields of hull barley and wheat, sown in November, bundled. Potatoes, cauliflower, buckwheat, soybeans, and onions filled the pastures, ripe at the end of June. Tomatoes were grown year-round in greenhouses along the river. There were fruit trees, apricots, peaches, 45 varieties of apples, and walnuts. Occasionally, dzo—cow-yak hybrid teams—plowed the fields. Himalayan blue pines, spruce, and juniper dotted the hillsides. Otherwise, there was little color or vegetation on the grey shale and the black scree (loose gravel that feels like rolling marbles when walked on).

Our group hiked up to a higher altitude during the day and slept at a lower altitude at night to help with acclimatization. We followed a pilgrimage circuit up to a promontory overlooking the Kali Gandaki to the 17th-century Kutsab Tergna ("The Five Treasures of Bodily Representation") temple believed to be the most sacred Tibetan Buddhist site in the Jomsom area. En route, we saw the ruins of Serib Garab Dzong (Joyour Fort), the fortress/palace of a kingdom that ruled the area for centuries until the 1700s. We were lucky to find the key keeper for the Bonpo temple and go inside.

After dinner, other guests staying in the same hotel used the center courtyard to play cards, party, and visit most of the night; we got in our sleeping bags but barely slept. The next morning, we walked through town and boarded jeeps to drive us up the riverbed. Arranging all this took time, so we waited nearly two hours until we started our approach to Kagbeni, the gateway into the restricted zone of Upper Mustang. Kag is said to mean "Block", an appropriate name for the strategic rocky outcrop where the Kali Gandaki River narrows. Fortresses to deter invaders have been situated here for over a thousand years, and the town is built like one. The route beyond Kagbeni through Mustang was a major trade route between India and Tibet for centuries, until the early 1960s following the Communist Chinese invasion of Tibet when Tibet's borders were sealed off from her neighbors. Since then, the caravans of traders have been retrofitted for adventurous trekkers. In more recent times, the buildings have been built to withstand the howling afternoon winds from the Tibetan Plateau more than to deter invaders.[12] Kagbeni seemed like a setting from a fairytale: a crumbling, turreted castle overlooked this ancient town, serenely surrounded by

---

[12] Wilderness Travel, Ultimate Mustang Itinerary, 2009, page 4

terraced greenery and trees in the parched landscape.[13]

Our drive was exciting, as the river necked down to a narrow channel along fields of grain surrounded by mud-plastered walls, ripening fruit trees, willows, and a crumbling fortress, built during the Dolpo-Mustang invasions, which easily controlled the trade routes between Tibet and India. There was a 500-year-old red ochre, three-story gompas, Tubten Sampeling, (a collection from monasteries) filled with wonderful wooden masks and hundreds of yak butter lanterns. Two over-life-sized erotic clay figurines marked the entrance to the town; they were anatomically correct statues of a male and female with an enormous erect penis and an opened vagina. They even had hair in the appropriate places. Gary did not have an answer as to their significance when we asked him. That night we stayed in a lodge before starting the trek the next day.

For the next three weeks, we'd camp. In order to shield us from the wind, our tents were always set up within a walled corral, usually on dirt. Each afternoon, our 20 mules and five ponies were unsaddled and removed from our space before we moved into all our campsites on the trek. Pauline and I shared one four-person Mountain Hardware tent,

---

[13] Wilderness Travel, Ultimate Mustang itinerary, 2010

and the emergency room doctor and his friend shared the other. The rest of our group members had single North Face VE25 tents. The tents were spacious and accommodated our duffels, which were limited to 33 pounds.

Whenever possible, our cook team raced ahead of us and found a spare room, maybe a villager's dining room, in one of the tiny, white-washed settlements we hiked through. There, they cooked a hot lunch that they served to us on a cloth-covered table while we sat on either benches or collapsable chairs to get out of the wind and sun. On our first day's five-hour roller coaster march, we arrived at Chuksang and settled into a lunch of carrot/radish salad, curried potatoes, slabs of ham, and fried bread.[14]

After lunch, the trail led us to a steep downhill covered in scree. I asked, "Gary, how do I walk on this?" "Just slide," he replied. All would have been perfect, except I skidded out and fell so hard on my right wrist that it broke. After I fell, I just lay there in shock. It all happened so fast, and I fell hard. Gary sat with me and thought I had sprained my wrist. I hoped he was correct, but my wrist was swollen and throbbing. I knew I could be helicoptered out and sent home to receive medical attention, but I didn't want to

---

[14]. Pauline Green, Two Tablespoons of Sugar, p.4

leave. This would probably be the only opportunity I had to do something like this; I'd gone through so many hoops to get this far, and I was already there.

From the moment I stood up, a guide was always with me and carried my day pack. A few days later, I thought I could carry my pack, and our Sardar (lead guide), Chundi Phurba Sherpa from Namche, just shook his head and took it out of my hands. Pauline graciously opened and closed our tent zipper which was often stuck because of all the dust caught in the tracks. Neither of us can remember how I tied my boots! A week later, Gary and the emergency room doctor wrapped my arm in a hard SAM splint, but it wasn't getting better. The doctor confided that he hadn't wanted to interfere with Gary's role; I was grateful that he stepped in to help.

When we hiked across the Kali Gandaki River, we entered an eerily beautiful world of eroded ancient ocean sediments, and kept our eyes open for ammonites, fossilized mollusks resembling a chambered nautilus—they're actually related to cuttlefish and squid—that lived over 100 million years ago, when this area was covered by the Tethys Sea, prior to the Indian subcontinent's collision with the Asian mainland. The Mustang ammonites are considered to be sacred earthly manifestations of Lord Vishnu, the god of truth and peace.[15]

---

[15] Wilderness Travel, Ultimate Mustang Itinerary, 2009, page 4

To Gary's credit, he'd studied anthropologist David Snellgrove's books on the origins of Buddhism and its subsequent migration into Tibet's culture, and those of Michel Peissel, a French adventurer who spent almost a year writing in Mustang in the early 1960s. Gary made sure we stopped at many of the famous Tibetan Buddhist monasteries and caves along our route. Most of our sherpas had never visited this, region and were visibly moved and appreciative of the religious aspects; so was I. One afternoon, while others went on an optional five-hour trek, I visited one of the oldest monasteries with several of our sherpas. Chundi found the villager who had the key. and we reverently entered the dimly lit monastery and walked along the perimeter past ancient frescoes of Buddhas and famous rinpoches towards the front. Large gold-plated Buddhas and religious artifacts with statues of ferocious beasts to protect them were located opposite the door where we entered. As sherpas took handfuls of rice to put in their pockets they explained to me that they would put this rice above the front doors to their homes for protection. I slipped some in my pocket to take home too. I treasure the memory of sharing this time with them.

Our days started when it was just getting light. One day as we gained elevation ascending 2,873 feet and approached Ghemi, to our surprise the King of Mustang's nephew, Rajah, rode out on his motorcycle to meet us. He was looking for a woman in our group, Lisa, the 40-year-old from Seattle, who worked in the financial arena. We didn't know it at the time, but she had contributed to one of Ghemi's nursery schools. Before leaving on this trip, she had mentioned to someone she would be in the region, and the news was relayed to Rajah. We were amazed that he found her, and he extended an invitation to our group for tea in his hotel.

Rajah and his wife have run a hotel in Ghemi for over 10 years. It sees mostly French tourists. Their two children were in Kathmandu for the school year, and their parents would join them in November. They spoke good English and had been to the East Coast in the States. His description of Manhattan, "Where everyone is running after time," made us laugh, because it is true! Because the internet and technological advances are happening so quickly, our nervous systems can't keep up and we feel like we never have enough time. Later, they opened their collection of antique piles of gorgeous Tibetan pony blankets, thankas (wall hangings), chang vessels (painted pottery), scripture tablets, belts, jewelry and rugs, which were all for sale. Purchases were made and later he rode his horse to the outskirts of Kathmandu, took a bus, and delivered our purchases to us in our hotel!

Before we left Ghemi, several of us visited the children in the nursery school. The children were shy and adorable. With their teacher's encouragement, they sang songs for us and placed khataks around our necks. In return, we sang "Itsy Bitsy Spider" while they stared at us as if we were creatures from Mars. As we turned to leave, I looked back and noticed the donor's eyes were filled with tears. She was deeply moved by the experience. It was one thing to write a check, and another completely different experience to be in the presence of these children.

As we continued our trek, we visited many chortens and monasteries. One of particular interest was Chyungsi Rhangchung Cave, found above a steep riverbed. We were told that Guru Rinpoche meditated here over 1,000 years ago. This means that this holy individual brought Indian Buddhism to the Mustang region while he was journeying to Tibet, where he founded Samye, Tibet's first monastery. Impressive Persian-like Sanskrit petroglyphs (rock engravings) were carved into the walls. This was the only cave we saw that had petroglyphs and murals. Today, an elderly monk and his granddaughter occupy the space as caretakers. Bricks sealed up much of the former opening and a small wood stove kept the couple warm at 11,500 feet. The visit was well worth the extra steps it took to get there[16].

---

[16] Wilderness Travel, Ultimate Mustang Itinerary, 2009, page 4

After five more hours of hiking and ascending another 2,644 feet through a dry barren wide landscape escorted by a grey mare and her foal, we walked through the entrance to Lo Manthang, one of the last walled cities in Asia. The 15th-century village of about 1,000 people is situated about 12 miles south of the Tibetan/Chinese border. Our campsite was in a grove of trees, surrounded by six-foot walls made of stone and mud. Lo Manthang is also the home of the elderly King, who invited us to his palace for tea one afternoon. We were served tea in his receiving room while the King on his throne dosed. Nevertheless, it was another interesting experience.

A highlight during our four-day stay in Lo Manthang was our visit to Jampa Lhakhang temple, with its extraordinary mandala wall murals, which were being restored by Luigi Fieni, the lively curator from Italy, and his team through a grant from the American Himalayan Foundation. Originally trained as an aeronautics engineer, he wanted to do something with his hands. One of his professors appreciated Luigi's ability to copy and invited him to join the project. This temple contains statues of Maitreya, a future Buddha, believed to be still in heaven in the state of a Bodhisattva. The name Maitreya means "benevolence" or "friendship". He is now living his last existence as a Bodhisattva, or being in the state of enlightenment. His arrival is imminent.[17]

Luigi explained that Nepalese and Tibetans living in the area believed he was the reincarnation of a lama who had painted there centuries before. There are over 20,000 sacred caves surrounding Lo Manthang. Many have been plundered and others remain hidden, even to Luigi. Before he and the artists being trained in restoration techniques begin to work on a fresco, a ceremony takes place to capture all the spirits from the paintings and place them in a container for safe keeping. One of his challenges was educating his Nepalese assistants about why it was important to preserve these treasures, which was against their belief of impermanence. For them, the souls in the art were important, not the art.

Each floor of the temple represents a different level of enlightenment. When we reached the fourth floor, Luigi explained that when this tantric/sutra zone was completely restored, it would only be open for the highest lamas, who have a deep understanding of its complex religious significance. After our tour, Luigi and his two Italian team members joined us for one of our most festive dinners on our trip. Our cook prepared a feast of sautéed spinach, potatoes, lamb chops, and a cake to celebrate the occasion.

---

[17] http://www.buddhanet.net/e-learning/history/maitreya2.htm

The next day, we rode in the back of a pick-up truck for a couple of hours across badlands to visit newly discovered cave temples with their wonderful circa thirteenth-century wall murals, which showed a distinct Newari influence in the art, a style different than any other art found in Mustang. Access to the caves required ropes and ladders to reach the entrances. Thanks to our sherpa's genuine interest and enthusiasm for this expedition, everyone made the climb to the caves. It was exhilarating to be in a place recently discovered and not yet visited by waves of tourists. We were the only ones there.

Before we left for the caves, Pauline and I laid out our cleanest clothes on top of our sleeping bags. By this point in the trek, we had sand everywhere on our clothes and bodies. All of us were ready for a shower, and an informal hierarchy in the group had been established. The day before, simple sun showers were offered to us, using water carried from a nearby stream, heated over a fire, poured into a bucket, and placed inside a small tent. The two older women stepped right up to have a shower while Pauline and I explored town to find a solar-powered shower we'd heard about from one of Luigi's assistants. While others took their camp showers, Pauline and I made a reservation in the only solar shower establishment in town, owned by an entrepreneurial young Tibetan woman who greeted us with a thriving, healthy nursing infant in her arms.

On the drive back from the caves, each of us exhausted and caked in dust, one of the women who had a sun shower the day before announced emphatically that she was going to take a solar shower. Before the words were out of her mouth, I stated even more emphatically that Pauline and I had made a reservation already. My comment upended the group hierarchy, made others pause, and gave us a competitive edge in the race to the solar showers. As soon as the truck stopped, the race was on. Since our clothes were on top of our sleeping bags, we easily beat our two competitors to the shower. Because the water was limited, Pauline and I agreed to take the shower together in a spacious shower stall, open to the sky, with hot water and good pressure. We laughed and howled with glee while washing our hair and ridding ourselves of dust accumulated over days. Pauline appreciated and couldn't get over the fact that I had spoken up as effectively as I had. I'd had enough and was incensed that the women felt so entitled after the staff had carried water for them the previous day. Fortunately, there was enough warm water for all of us.

We next discovered that the emergency room doctor and his companion unexpectedly decided to leave the trek. They left our group on the last truck to Jomsom via the only (newly built) road, soon to be washed out by the monsoons. This was a surprise to the rest of us. In spite of their politics, we enjoyed their presence and talking to them. As they said quick goodbyes to each of us, the doctor explained he didn't think he was fit enough for the next leg of our journey, and his friend worried about having respiratory problems because of the dust and increasing altitude. Sadly, we waved goodbye as they piled onto the back of the truck, filled with other passengers, chickens, goats, and one of our sherpas, who rejoined us a couple of days later.

On this trek and in subsequent treks I've led, the guides never left any group members on their own to fend for themselves. The guides took their jobs seriously and felt responsible for us while we were with them. After leaving Lo Manthang, we had many eight-to-ten-hour trekking days and crossed several passes varying between 16,000 and 18,400 feet on our way to Damodar Kund, the Holy Lake. We crossed a couple of rivers; for one particular crossing, Lama, one of our sherpas, gallantly carried the women across on his back.

En route, we passed a couple of traditional sky burial sites. Tibetans believe in the transformation of spirits, and so there is no need to preserve the body, as it is now an empty vessel. Jhator, or sky burial, means "giving alms to the birds." First, the monks carry the deceased's body to the crest of the nearest hill. Two men serve as rogyapas, translated as "body breakers." The stomach is slit open as vultures begin to circle the site. When the birds have consumed most of the flesh, the rogyapas crush the bones and mix them with tsampa, barley flour mixed with salty yak butter, to spur the vultures on. When only the skull remains, the men shatter it with a mortar and pestle, mix the bones and brain matter together, and put the offering on a stone while vultures circle, making an eerie cry. Usually, the largest black vulture consumes the remains. The belief is that if all the remnants are consumed, a reincarnation of the deceased will occur.[18] We didn't actually see one of these burials, but these sites felt sacred and more than that. The simplicity of the ritual, how it embodies the culture and reverence for life, was palpable.

It was slow going because of the increasing altitude and our frequent breaks, when we'd all lie flat on the ground, exhausted. Along the way, Pauline ate spoonfuls of peanut butter (Jif Extra Crunchy was her brand) right out of the jar. Others had hard candies, power bars, and chocolate, often melted into the paper. Some mornings, we had our bed tea at 4:30 or 5 a.m. and were on the trail by 6:15 to get as far as we could before covering our faces with dust masks to protect ourselves from the 30-mile-per-hour winds blowing dust and gravel. Most days we gained three or four thousand feet in altitude, to discover another ridge to climb. We walked along ridges that were like

---

[18] p.164, Relin, Second Sons

gentle roller coasters, and it seemed like we were on top of the world and as if we'd walk right out over the ridge. We were thrilled when we saw blue sheep, soaring eagles, and vultures. By the time we entered camp for the evening, we were caked with sweat and dust. It was a treat if there was enough water in a spring or a farmer's hose where we could wash. As challenging as our days were, we reveled in the silence, routine, and peace surrounding us.

In addition to a jar of peanut butter, Pauline carried her mother's ashes the whole way to the Holy Lake, looking for the spot to toss them into the wind. She chose an 18,400-foot pass after we had just seen glaciated Dhaulagiri to the north, now only 9,000 feet above us. Around a barren corner, we saw the Damodar Himal mountain range between us and the Chinese border (about six miles to the east). From this ridge, because of tricks in the atmosphere, it looked like we could toss stones across to Tibet. In this sacred place, Pauline tied three new prayer scarves (one from Lama, one from the King of Mustang, and one from his nephew) to the stake at the top of a primitive chorten, marking the summit of the pass. Faded tattered prayer flags fluttered above her as she unwrapped a small Kashmir box and tossed her mother's ashes to the winds. She felt elated, exhilarated, and sad all at the same time. Her mother had read *Scientific American* and talked about the topography, geology, plate tectonics, and fossils she had studied, which were much like those of this sacred place. She had always wanted to go there, but wouldn't when Pauline offered to take her because she didn't want to leave her husband.

As we neared the Holy Lake, it became apparent that the only person who knew where it was located happened to be our mule herder. If it hadn't been for him, our cook, Bakhat, and our competent, skilled, physically strong, conscientious, highly intuitive sherpas—Rai, from Solu, our sherpa leader, Chundi, and Phura Sherpa from Namche—I would have been terrified. But I knew they would always find water and a place to camp for us. Many days we walked 10 to 12 hours to make sure we reached water near camp. Since it was an exploratory trip, Gary—who hadn't actually been to the Holy Lake—had fortunately hired this staff, and took meticulous notes for his next book. By the time we left the lake, Pauline called it "the muddy pond."

One night, feeling more exhausted than other days, I left the dining tent right after dinner to see Chundi standing with a cup in his hand, watching the mule herder and his assistants race on foot out of camp. I asked him what happened, and he explained the mules had escaped and were going home! I continued to my tent and assumed Chundi would let Gary know, since Gary often talked about his good relationships with them.

The next morning, after Gary outlined our plans, I quietly asked if he knew the mules had run away. He was chagrined to admit that he didn't know. Since the mules were gone, we had a change of plans. Instead of leaving early, we had to wait until the mules returned to camp. We left after lunch to hike back over the high passes and started our descent to the riverbed campsite. If it hadn't been for Bakat, who met us at the highest pass carrying tea and cookies with a wide grin, a few of us might not have made it back over the two high passes all the way to camp. Each time I crossed a pass, I sent blessings and prayers to my family members and for world peace, placed a stone on the chortan as I walked around it, gazed out over the vast landscape, and soaked in the sacred energy of the place and moment.

On our way down, emaciated sadhus (holy men) marched by in loincloths, and streams of pilgrims without supplies or ponies passed us en route to the lake that we found underwhelming. They were traveling without food and supplies to the Lake to honor Vishnu. Vishnu's earthly incarnations have many avatars. His ten avatars are Matsyavatara (fish), Koorma (tortoise), Varaaha (boar), Narasimha (the man-lion), Vaamana (the dwarf), Parasurama (the angry man), Lord Rama (the perfect human of the Ramayana), Lord Balarama (Krishna's brother), Lord Krishna (the divine diplomat and statesman), and the yet-to-appear 10th incarnation called the Kalki avatar. Some sources consider Buddha as one of the avatars of Vishnu.[19]

About midday, while we were stretched out on the ground taking a break, Luigi and his entourage—like a carnival, on ponies, and in good moods—met us en route to the Holy Lake that Gary had encouraged them to see. Seeing them lifted our spirits considerably. When we reached camp later that day, the mules and ponies were back.

By the time we reached Jomson, our guides had managed to turn on the hot water for the rooms, and we were able to shower and clean up before our final dinner. Bakat made sure we were overindulged with soup, roast chicken, pizza, salad, potatoes, two bottles of wine, beer, and an apple cake with "welcome" written in the frosting! We toasted and tipped the entire staff including pony boys, our beloved cook's crew and sherpas, and Sidar. What an incredible group of guys! Since we didn't have contact with regional people, it was this crew that left a warm, gracious, helpful, and wonderful impression on us.[20]

This trek was even more difficult than I imagined. It was also the most fascinating trip I've

---

[19] http://hinduism.about.com/od/godsgoddesses/p/vishnu.htm

[20] , Pauline Green, Two Tablespoons of Sugar, p. 8

ever taken. There were many highlights, including the caves, spectacular scenery, magical communities, grand vistas, and strenuous terrain. Often I felt ecstatically happy, and I never felt afraid for my safety because of our sherpas, the strongest, calmest, most competent people I ever met. In spite of the physical hardship, I can still feel in my bones what it was like to be in such a remote sacred place, to pass devotees walking in bare feet and little clothing, turbans wrapped around their heads, to reach a holy site. I loved how it felt to be lying on the ground under a clear blue sky on the Tibetan plateau, listening to the lulling chimes of the bells tied around our pack animal's necks, and the sound of their hooves on the dirt as they made their way slowly up and down the steep terrain. I felt transported and loved being in nature at high altitudes near Tibet.

Once we finished our trek and returned to the Shangri-La Hotel in Kathmandu, Pauline and I took turns in the shower scrubbing off 24 days of dust. We happily changed into the clean clothes we'd left in extra suitcases at the hotel. Our grungy clothes and filthy socks were stuffed into our duffel bags lined with plastic garbage bags, to be soaked and washed several times once we were home. While we rested and showered, the others couldn't wait to get to Fire and Ice Café—a popular restaurant for American tourists—for french fries, hamburgers, and milkshakes. After our showers, Pauline and I returned to one of my favorite pashmina stores. We marveled at how happy and peaceful we felt just sitting on a couch, watching our saleswomen carefully and slowly fold and wrap my purchase of a pashmina I bought for my daughter.

After saying goodbye to the rest of the group, Pauline and I spent the night with the Websters in their lodge, the same place I'd visited after the trek to the Everest region years before. Steve showed us a hotel I might use if I brought a group next year. We were served ice-cubed lemonade with fresh mint when we arrived; and, after cocktails on the terrace, had a lovely salmon, asparagus and mashed potato dinner. Their 12-year-old daughter, Priyani, played her guitar and sang songs for us. It was a truly relaxed, charming evening with fireflies and cuckoo birds. When Pauline and I said goodbye to each other, I wasn't sure we'd even stay in touch since she lived in Denver. It reassured me when her partner Mo explained that Pauline is a really good friend and would stay in touch.

My trip home thru Delhi, with my arm wrapped in a filthy ace bandage held in a kaftan sling, was an experience. There were two highlights: One, a young man who was an EMT working in Rockville, Maryland (five miles from my home) had just completed a long trek with a buddy. He kindly offered to wrap my arm after observing me wrapping and unwrapping it myself. Second, after what seemed like days of waiting for my flight and being shuffled from one waiting area to another, I went thru security. The young security guard insisted I unwrap my arm. An older Indian woman standing behind me, dressed in an elaborate sari and beautiful jewelry, admonished our young security guard for insisting I unwrap my arm. Nevertheless, I had to unwrap it.

Seeing a doctor about my arm was a priority once I got home. Luckily, it was set without any complications. I wore a cast for several weeks, followed by physical therapy appointments for several more. I'll never forget the look on my boss's face when I returned with a broken arm. She wasn't impressed. Mentally, I had already given notice at work before I left for Mustang. After I returned, I was out of the office as much as I could be. The next big step was to submit my resignation. The political climate made it easier for me to resign. Plus, my physical health was taking a toll—I started breaking out in hives from the stress at my job.

Nevertheless, I felt like I was jumping off a cliff when I submitted my resignation. It was difficult and sad to say goodbye to clients and colleagues, but not to leave my job. Once I left, I was disoriented without the structure and security of a regular routine and paycheck. This surprised me, since I continued to work in my private practice, was President of the Greater Washington Society of Clinical Social

Workers, and began spending more time marketing my first voluntourism trip to Nepal.

The feeling of emptiness those first few Mondays was terrifying. My schedule seemed empty. I couldn't imagine how I'd fill the week. After a couple of months, en route to the gym, one of my friends asked me how I was feeling. She said, "Sydney, you are happy; this is happy." I realized she was right. Six months later, I woke up one morning without a knot in my stomach and that urgent feeling that I already was late and already behind. I gradually settled into a comfortable routine.

Meanwhile, I practiced my speech about the trek in Toastmasters, and spoke to small groups in a yoga studio, a women's dress store, friends' homes, wherever I could. Six months later, three brave baby boomers registered to join our first trip. To my delight, Pauline and I talked regularly, and she offered to reassure my clients and answer questions for them about socks, boots, poles, and anything to do with equipment. My outlandish idea was becoming a reality.

PART III—My Outlandish Idea Worked! How We Did It

Chapter 11—Religious Holidays

After years of dreaming my idea into life, I led the group consisting of three courageous women who joined the first Trek of Your Life voluntourism trip to Nepal in October 2011. Since then, I've taken groups back yearly (except during COVID), over 120 people including sisters, mother-daughter duos, father-son duos, married couples, and single men and women between the ages of 23-84 years old.

We basically followed the same itinerary until 2015, the year of the Gorkha earthquake with a magnitude of 7.6 and more than 300 aftershocks. Every year, group members would be met after they arrived at the airport, and accompanied to the hotel where they would spend two nights. Until 2015, the next four nights were spent at Shivapuri Heights Cottage. While we were there, Steve and Neeru facilitated our volunteer service time nearby in Dadagaun Village. Our projects in the school, clinic, and orphanage have been sustainable because other groups like ours return each year; Christine and her husband Kurt spent several months there yearly, and Steve and Neeru monitored progress on a regular basis. Even though the itinerary has been the same each year, each group has had a life of its own because of the needs in the village and our members' skills—teachers, nurses, accountants, computer wizards, lawyers and social workers contribute their time and experience. They taught English, accounting, crafts, and how to make washable feminlne products so the girls can go to school. They set up and maintained the computer room; donated a sewing machine, a printer, and ink for the printer; helped start the women's group; and taught them how to make compost to sell along with organic vegetables and flowers. Group members have donated money for new printers and paid for 36 children to attend high school. (Public education is only mandatory through seventh grade.) Their enjoyment, feedback, and continuing enthusiasm inspired each of us. One of the teacher-volunteers said, "What we are doing for the children is everlasting."

Those who have chosen to travel with me risk changing how they see the world and themselves. Many have joined me more than once. Each time we have gone, I witnessed moving personal transformations and have been inspired by how open-minded people change their priorities, increase their capacity for relating to others, and contribute to something bigger than themselves. It is commonly known now that such actions are the source of true happiness.

Late October and November are the best months to visit Nepal, for two reasons. First, the weather is relatively stable, warm, and sunny during the day and cool at night. Second, one of two major religious holidays typically occurs, depending on Nepal's many minor community calendars— particularly the Bikram Sambat calendar[21] based on ancient Hindu tradition, which is 56.7 years ahead of the solar Gregorian calendar. Nepalese religious and spiritual practices enhance our cultural experience and appreciation because they are interwoven into daily life.

One of the major holidays is Tihar, commonly known as the festival of lights. It begins the thirteenth day of the waning moon, and is one of the most dazzling of all Hindu festivals. Prosperity and wealth are celebrated for five days. Each day has a different name and celebrates a different aspect or god. One sacred day honors the Goddess Laxmi, the goddess of wealth and the wife of almighty Lord Vishnu, the lord of peace and order on earth. According to Hindu beliefs, she was formed from the ocean. Images of her sitting on a full-grown lotus or on her owl can be

---

[21] http://en.wikipedia.org/wiki/Krishna

seen in temples and along the streets of Kathmandu. Yamaraj, lord of death and the underworld, is also worshipped in different forms during this holiday.[22] One of the legends explaining why Tihar is celebrated so widely involves a king living his last days of life. His astrologer told him that a serpent would come and take his life. The king did not want to die, and asked the astrologer if there was any way to escape death. He was advised to sleep with lit oil lamps all around his bed, and to decorate the palace with oil lamps on Laxmi puja (prayer) day because she could convince the serpent not to take the king's life. The serpent took the king to Yamaraj and told him that it was not yet the king's time to go to the underworld. Upon hearing this, Yamaraj opened his ledger where the king's remaining time was written as zero, but the serpent cleverly put a seven before it. Thus, the king lived for 70 more years.[23]

The first day of Tihar is known as Kag Tihar, or Crow's Day. In the morning before humans eat, food is offered to the crows on a plate made of leaves. They are sacred because, according to legend, one crow happened to drink from the water of life (sacred water). They are not afraid of humans and can be

---

[22] Avigya Karki, The Nepalese Traditions: Festivals in Nepal, 1998. www.nepalhomepage.com

[23] Ibid

---

seen sitting calmly everywhere. Crows are honored as the messenger of death.[24]

The second day of the festival is called Kukur Tihar, or Dog's Day. Dogs play many roles. Nepalese pray to a divine dog to guard their house the same way the dog guards the gate of the underworld, diverting destruction. According to another legend, an ordinary dog intervened to save his master's life, offering to be killed instead of his owner. Shiva, in his fear-invoking aspect Bhairav, rides on a dog. To honor the dogs, a big red tika (a combination of rice-dyed red and flour paste) is put on the dog's forehead, and a beautiful marigold garland is placed around its neck. After the dog is worshipped, it is given a meal of milk and cookies. In Nepal, especially on this day, the saying "every dog has his day" is verified, because even a stray dog is regarded with respect.[25]

The third day of the festival is the day Laxmi is worshipped. It is believed that at the stroke of midnight, Laxmi makes a world tour on her owl to see how she was worshipped. Early on this same day, cows—the symbol of wealth, the holiest animal for Hindus and the national animal for Nepal—are also worshipped. Tika is placed on the cow's forehead, a

---

[24] Ibid.

[25] Ibid.

---

marigold garland around its neck, and fed fresh hay and grains, delicious food for a cow.[26]

The fourth day of the holiday varies, depending on the cultural background of the Nepalese. Most perform Guru puja, or ox worshiping, as they worship the cow with tika, a garland, and then a feast. Those who follow Lord Krishna, the eighth reincarnation of Vishnu,[27] perform Gobhardhan puja. Pujas are prayer rituals worshiping life. This puja is practiced by building a small hill out of cow dung and burning some grass on it while saying a prayer. This symbolizes the act of Lord Krishna when he lifted Gobhardhan Hill, saving millions of people and cows from floodwater. Members of the Newar community perform Mha puja to celebrate one's essence, to cleanse and empower the soul to begin the New Year.[28]

The last day of Tihar is Bhai Tika, the day sisters honor their brothers by placing tika on their foreheads and praying to Yamaraj. In practice, on the day before, Nepal's royal astrologer announces on the radio the appropriate time to place tika on their brother's foreheads. All brothers in Nepal receive tika

---

[26] Ibid.

[27] http://en.wikipedia.org/wiki/Krishna

[28] Aviga; op.cit

at the same time, even the King, who is accompanied by a 31-gun salute.[29]

According to Vedic tradition, Yamaraj was considered to have been the first mortal who died and traveled the celestial abodes to become the ruler of the dead. Yama is also the lord of justice and is sometimes referred to as Dharma, for his unswerving dedication to maintaining order and harmony during his brother's long life.

The other major holiday that occasionally occurs while we would visit (October-November) is Dashain, a 15-day-long national religious festival. It is highly anticipated, celebrated worldwide, and considered the most auspicious festival in the Nepalese annual calendar. During this holiday, many people trek for several days and travel long distances to visit their families, as well as renew community ties in remote villages. People return from all parts of the world, as well as different parts of the country, to celebrate together. All government offices, educational institutions, and other offices remain closed during the festival period.

Dashain celebrates Laxmi, in all her various forms. It begins with the bright lunar fortnight and ends on the day of the full moon. In 2013, while we were volunteering at the Dadagaun orphanage, we

---

[29] Aviga; op.cit

101

were honored to be included in the ritual practiced on the last day of Dashain. We lined up after the children to bow our heads on one side of the table with a brass plate holding tika, small bundles of grass (representing harvest) and a pile of ten rupee bills (ten cents in US currency) symbolizing abundance. One by one, we were blessed by Ramesh, the children's "father". Then we were served a special holiday dinner of dahl, goat, and greens in the dining room.

Chapter 12—Sightseeing, Recreation, and Relaxation

For the first four years, I happily returned to the Shangri-La Hotel two days before group members to rest, have a massage, have meetings, and visit my favorite cashmere shops. During the first years, I waited at the airport with Steve's reliable driver, Arjune. One year, the traffic was so congested I worried we'd never get there on time, but we always did. After Arjune dropped me off, I sat in the waiting room until he turned up right beside me after he parked the car. In the crowded, no-frills waiting room, sitting on old metal chairs, we looked through a smudged glass window for weary American travelers to arrive.

After the long journey to Nepal (about 34 hours) each person was relieved and delighted to greet us. With smiles all around, we loaded up the car and drove about 15 minutes through Kathmandu to the Hyatt Hotel. Once through the Hyatt gates, our exhausted travelers took a sigh of relief. We spent our first two nights there so that everyone had a chance to adjust to the unfamiliar surroundings. One member of our group greeted me saying, "Sydney, this is just like the book *Eat, Pray, Love*." She was delighted with her room, the food, the garden, the architecture, and the interior design. After everyone settled in, there was often time to walk out the back gates of the Hyatt garden along cobblestone streets, past monasteries, to Boudhanath.

Boudhanath, the largest Buddhist stupa outside of Tibet, is designated as a Unesco World Heritage Site. It is over 2,000 years old. Stupas are structures built to resemble mounds and contain Buddhist relics. Today, around 20,000 Tibetan refugees live in Nepal; many practice and live in monasteries around the stupa.

Eric Weiner, a *New York Times* travel writer, wrote an article about his visit to spiritual sites in the world. He described Boudhanath as the "thinnest place in the world. The place where heaven and earth are closest together. It is a place," he wrote, "where open-minded people feel divine influences directly exerted on their souls."[30] My experience deepened each time I visited.

For the first four years, Steve and I worked together. After our visit to Boudhanath, Steve joined us for an early dinner to give an orientation and answer any questions. The next morning, we enjoyed breakfast from a bountiful buffet of typical Western, European, and Eastern food, in elegant surroundings

---

[30] Eric Weiner," Where Heaven and Earth Come Closer," *New York Times*, March 9, 2012.

on the terrace overlooking the garden and pool, with a view of Boudhanath over the garden wall.

Our guide for the day and Steve's assistant, Sohan, met us in the lobby for a day of sightseeing. He is Newari, the group indigenous to Kathmandu Valley, and quite knowledgeable about Nepal's history, Hinduism, and Buddhism.

Our first stop was Pashupatinath Temple, the oldest Hindu temple in Kathmandu, dating back to 400 AD, built in the Nepalese pagoda style of architecture. Cubic brick constructions were used and rested on beautifully carved wooden rafters. The two-level roofs are made of copper with gold covering. It has four main doors, each covered with silver sheets and a gold pinnacle (Gajur), which is a symbol of religious thought. In front of the western door, there is a statue of a large bull or Nandi, plated in bronze. This deity is of black stone, about six feet in height and the same in circumference.

Several complex legends have been created around the origins of Pashupatinath. One involves Shiva and Parvati, who came to Kathmandu Valley and rested by the Bagmati River while on a journey. Shiva was so impressed by its beauty and the surrounding forest, that he and the Goddess Parvati transformed themselves into deer and walked into the forest. Many spots in the Kathmandu Valley are identified as places Shiva went during his time as a deer. After a while, the people and gods began to search for Shiva. Finally, after various complications, they found him in the forest, but he refused to leave. More complications ensued, but ultimately Shiva announced that since he had lived by the Bagmati in a deer's form, he would now be known as Pashupatinath, Lord of all Animals. It is said that whoever came here and beheld the lingam (a penis-shaped representation of Shiva) would not be reborn as an animal.[31]

Another legend involves Parvati's incarnation as Sati, the Hindu goddess of marital felicity and longevity, who gave up her life because her father didn't respect Shiva. Grieved at losing her, Shiva wandered the world carrying her body. Wherever pieces of her body fell, temples were established, including one at Guhyeshwari, adjoining the Pashupatinath complex. Only Hindus are permitted in the temple, but we were allowed to view the cremation piers and temple buildings from across the river.

We saw families sitting on straw mats on the bank of the Ganges, eating the sacred Nepalese meal on large banana leaves in honor of their deceased family members. Meanwhile, the deceased's body would be wrapped in cloth with oils used for cremation on a pyre outside the temple near

---

[31] http://en.wikipedia.org/wiki/Pashupatinath_Temple

the river. Rice is placed on the pyre so the soul won't be hungry while traveling and prayers are chanted to speed the person to their next reincarnation. The body is covered with straw, to shield the family from seeing their loved one disintegrate. Clarified butter from a golden urn is poured through the thin shroud covering the face, into the open mouth until it overflows and spills down the person's cheeks. According to their practices, the oldest child in the family lights the fire in the holiest place, the mouth, for the cremation. Finally, the ashes are poured into the river, completing the cycle of life. It is believed human bodies are made of the elements: air, earth, water, fire, and metal.[32] Metal is an addition to the more usual four.

We always visited one of the three Durbar Squares. Dubar Square is the generic name used to describe plazas and areas opposite the old royal palaces. Before Nepal was unified, it was a region of small kingdoms, each with a Durbar Square. Today, they are the most prominent remnants of those old kingdoms. The three most famous Durbar Squares in Kathmandu Valley are Kathmandu Durbar Square, Patan Durbar Square, and Bhaktapur Durbar Square. Each square consists of temples, idols, open courts,

---

[32] David Oliver Relin, *Second Sons*, p.234

water fountains, and more. All three are Unesco World Heritage sites.

After sightseeing, we walked through Thamel, the medieval historic district, exploring hidden corners of fabled Kathmandu. The ancient past lingers on in a maze of narrow streets crowded with turmeric sellers, small golden temples, wandering cows, and traditional workshops. The streets are tiny, busy, and crowded! Sohan insisted we stay closely together, as our senses were bombarded by bright colors and different smells of fruit, vegetables, animals, spices and incense. After our walk, Sohan left us to enjoy a late lunch on our own.

One of my favorite places for lunch was in the Garden of Dreams. What a relief to walk into the peaceful, neo-classical garden also known as the Garden of Six Seasons, created by late Field Marshal Kaiser Shumsher Rana. Built in the 1920s, it was considered one of the most sophisticated private gardens of that time but had been lying dormant for many years. Its renovation was handed over to the Austrian Government and implemented by Eco Himal. This model project has become a sustainable historic site, and a wonderful example of how historic places can be restored and developed.

After lunch, we returned to our hotel to rest before Sohan met us in the lobby for an evening tour of Boudhanath. This is a lovely time to visit, because it is prayer time for hundreds of Tibetan pilgrims.

Depending on which holiday is occurring, the stupa may be covered with colored lights. Our day, which was stimulating throughout, culminated under an evening sky and the welcome of total relaxation.

Chapter 13—Shivapuri and Volunteering

Before we left for Shivapuri Heights Cottage, a few group members and I would return to Boudhanath before breakfast. This was a lovely time to visit Boudhanath before the stores opened, and we joined the humble pilgrims silently circumambulating the stupa clockwise three times, spinning the prayer wheels, and turning them as we slowly walked. Our pace, the smell of incense, the clickety-clack of prayer wheels, the soft murmurs of mantras, the clanking of store shutters being opened, the colorful prayer flags, and the chortle of spoken Tibetan are mesmerizing. Even the brown, scraggly street dogs curled up on the street seem peaceful.

After joining the others for breakfast and checking out of our hotel, Arjun drove us for about 30 minutes to Steve and Neeru's lodge in the foothills above Kathmandu Valley. After 20 minutes on paved roads, we reached the foothills, leaving the colorful, lively, congested streets behind us. Some of us walked from this point, eager to stretch our legs. At the end of the steep, rutted dirt road leading to the cottage, we walked up the short steep path through the property gate to Shivapuri and continued for a few more minutes to our cottage.

Steve and Neeru welcomed us with smiles as they handed us glasses of cool lemonade topped with a sprig of fresh mint. Shivapuri, surrounded by urban forest, never failed to delight with its cottages, organic gardens, solar paneling, comfortable rooms, and million-dollar views of Kathmandu Valley. The food is fresh, prepared by BJ, their cook, who is like a family member, having worked there for so many years. Other staff members are warm and gracious. Usually we stayed in Jasmine cottage, which has three bedrooms, three baths, a dining/living room, and a small kitchen. There is another cottage nearby with one bedroom. Depending on how many are in our group, we used two bedrooms in the main house, built higher on the hill above Jasmine Cottage.

After settling, we had the option to visit Dadagaun Village and the Shanti Health Clinic where we volunteered. Some opted to stay in the cottage to rest, read or write, while others visited the village to get the lay of the land and talked about our service project.

Before our first visit each time, hours of planning and collaboration occurred between the school, the Websters, Christine and me to match the needs of the village with our group members' interests and skills. Steve was adamant that, until I had a group together, he wouldn't begin preparing our project for fear of disappointing the Nepalese people in the village.   After a brief tour of the sites, we visited a temple within walking distance of Shivapuri. If we were lucky, we arrived at prayer time and saw impish young monks in their robes chanting or playing in the courtyard. Afterward, we took a leisurely hike back on steep trails past homes surrounded by gardens, pots of marigolds, chickens, goats, and family members busy doing laundry, cooking, or gardening while their children played nearby. It felt good to get some exercise and an introduction to hiking in Nepal.

Steve built a fire on the patio in front of our cottage on the first night of our first trip. While we sat around the fire engaged in lively conversation, Steve reminded me of the meeting we had with Rinpoche Tezin Jango years before. I was stunned that I had forgotten. Steve shared the memory that even though he had taken many groups to Tengboche, our meeting was the only time he was invited to meet with the Rinpoche Tezin Jangpo. Since then, Steve has given each member of each group he has led on a trek a small Buddha and shared our conversation with the Rinpoche. I realized then that my experience may have planted a seed that gave me the idea for my voluntourism trips. Carolyn, a lawyer and a nurse who was in the first group, said, "I'll remember this trip for a very long time. It was an amazing experience. One I'll never forget."

Most of our meals were eaten with other guests on the terrace surrounding the main house or in the dining room. The entire first floor has two living rooms and a dining room which are open for guests to use. Until I grew accustomed to the nine-hour-and-fifteen-minute time difference between Nepal and the States, I woke before dawn, sat quietly, gazed out at Kathmandu Valley, and wrote in my journal until Tensing (the house boy) arrived carrying his day pack. After greeting me, he quietly turned off the small night lights around the room before going into the kitchen to boil water. He prepared a tray for us with cups, tea, coffee, sugar and milk, and placed the tray on a small table near the terrace. I soaked in the peaceful atmosphere and fresh air, while I gazed out over the valley, sipped tea, and listened to the birds and insects, waking up. Their chirping was an astounding contrast to those on the East Coast. It sounded like a symphony in comparison.

At 7 a.m., our yoga teacher, Rapesh Joshi, always arrived to teach Hatha yoga on the soft spongy green lawn beside our cottage. In the cool morning air under a clear blue sky, Rapesh gently led us through our poses surrounded by wild poinsettias, morning glories, jasmine, crickets, cuckoo birds, and the scent of wood burning. After class, we felt stretched, balanced, and peaceful. Rupesh joined us for breakfast and gave us an opportunity to ask questions. His training included three months in

Tirvandhanpur, India in one of the oldest Hatha yoga training centers in the world. Hatha focuses on using gentle poses and breathing to connect the mind, body, and spirit. A perfect way to start our day.

After breakfast of scrambled eggs, toast, fruit, and yogurt, we walked down the hill to meet Arjune, who drove us to Dadagaun Village. If we had doctors or nurses in our group, we visited Shanti Health Clinic, where people with leprosy and their families live and get treatment. The compound has family living quarters, organic gardens, a school, and a workroom for weaving and sewing. One of the most fascinating things to me were the round bricks, like big donuts, drying on a stick between two poles, like a clothesline. The bricks are made from soaking recycled paper and sawdust to be sold in Kathmandu for fuel. Each brick burns for an hour. The clinic sustains itself by selling these bricks and textiles in Kathmandu.

On our tour, we learned that leprosy can be cured, but leaves deep caverns in victims' deformed limbs that need to be cleaned and dressed regularly. One of the assistants trained us to clean and dress wounds. It is a simple process and completely safe. We wore surgical gloves and used clean bandages. Our apprehensions quickly melted away because the patients were friendly, warm, and appreciative. One of the women proudly introduced me to her two boys, who happily played marbles nearby with stones in the dirt yard while I cleaned her wound. Our non-verbal communication overcame our language barrier.

It was impressive to see how organized and professional the clinic was. Even the files were orderly and well-maintained. The Nepalese doctor, trained in Pakistan, explained that if people would wash their hands with soap regularly, 85% of the illnesses he treated would be cured, just like in the Western countries. Soap was expensive for this village, and education about how the disease is transmitted is needed. At the end of our day, we were served tea made of cardamon and basil to thank us.

Once while Neeru, our facilitator and translator, and I walked back to the jeep, she told me she was inspired by our group and loved spending time with us. I was surprised and encouraged to hear this. Each year, Neeru grew more confident; she carved out a role for herself. Our work in the village was effective because of her planning and her grace as a facilitator, translator, and photographer.

If Tihar is being celebrated, Shivapuri staff prepare for the evening festivities by carefully laying flower petals in beautiful designs leading to altars dedicated to Laxmi, surrounded by candles and flowers, in the cottage where we were staying and the main house while we volunteered. They start preparing days before, because houses are cleansed and decorated to please the goddess, who prefers clean and tidy places. In the evening, a small portion of the house outside the main door is painted with red mud and an oil lamp hung above it, illuminating a marigold petal pathway leading to the puja (prayer) room where the old money box and valuables are kept. Most Nepalese have a box handed down through generations, containing money added to it throughout the year worshipping goddess Laxmi. This money is saved for extreme emergencies.

Depending on our project, Steve oriented us and provided information on the school and orphanage. In our first year, we used questionnaires written by Steve, Christine and Dorje, the school principal, to survey the villagers in Dadagaun in their homes. The questionnaire was designed to determine what kind of support they wanted for themselves and their village. Dadagaun's special educational project was founded in the town in May 2010 by two couples from Australia, Christine and Kurt Marschner and Tony and Raewyn Morgan. Each year we had a different project, depending on the needs of the village. Naturally, the first year we were especially apprehensive and didn't know what to expect, since none of us had ever done anything like this before. After a 30-minute drive over rough roads, we reached Dadagaun Village. From this point, we walked since there weren't any roads in the village, just footpaths. Often our first stop was to meet the school principal, Dorje, in his home. He was 18 years old when he accepted the job as a school principal.

He welcomed us, and his wife prepared tea over the little fire pit in the well-swept dirt-floor kitchen of their mud brick cottage. We sat on a mud brick wall in the warm sunshine while Neeru and Dorje planned our day. Goats and chickens wandered in the tiny yard, the same goats and chickens who slept with the grizzly old dog in the kitchen "annex" overnight. The household tap to pump cold water was outside, just near the traditional style outhouse. There was no electricity or running water. His home was typical in this village.

The year we interviewed the villagers, Dorje translated for two of us, and Neeru translated for me and another social worker. After Neeru observed how I interviewed, she took the lead during our interviews. I was thrilled. After all, she is Nepalese and lives there. We walked through the village from home to home, interviewing villagers about what they would like next in their village, and gauging their reactions to foreigners like us. Once we started, our apprehensions just melted away. The villagers were open, warm, happy, grounded, and interested in us. Generally, we learned the villagers have farms and jobs that sustain them. Overall, they are healthy, thriving, and have few material things.

We witnessed many memorable scenes. One was a young mother massaging her plump infant son with sesame oil on a mat outside her front door as we walked by. Another mother, 24 years old, moved both

Neeru and me to tears. During our interview, she told us she was home because she had cut her leg badly as she carried wood on her back through the woods. When we asked what she hoped for her year-old baby girl, she said, "I will do whatever I have to make sure that she could go to school." At first, she was confused when we asked what she would like for herself. With our encouragement, she explained that she loved school and stopped when she was 12 years old because her sister got married, and she was expected to stay home to take care of her parents and work on the farm. She added, "If I could have adult education, I would do whatever I needed to do to learn. I would like to learn to be a tailor." When asked, "What is it like to have Westerners like us visit you?" She answered, "When people who seem as sincere as you and come so far, it makes me feel proud of my village, and like I can do more for myself." Her sincerity and determination were inspiring.

Through the years, each volunteer is always deeply touched and transformed by how warmly and enthusiastically we are received and appreciated. The experience allows us to tap into a universal energy that is transformative, reminding us of how good it feels to be connected to others and to ourselves, and offering a new perspective on our own culture.

This time, after a few hours, we had lunch at a nearby restaurant and returned to the village for a couple more hours. After resting in our cottage after volunteering, we joined other guests and family members for dinner. Throughout the evening, groups of girls visited and sang songs praising Laxmi. These girls were welcomed as guests and given gifts. Even gambling is legal during festivals. To the delight of the children and adults, Steve lit fireworks he purchased in China. Merriment lasted throughout the night.

The next morning, I had what seemed like a revelation to me. While I gazed at Kathmandu Valley, it dawned on me that I didn't need to wait for the house boy to boil water for tea. I could go into the small kitchen, light a match, and boil the water before anyone else was awake. When I reflected on this, I realized I had been in a dream state and was reminded of how totally different life is in Nepal. While I was contemplating, the sun rose and I was enveloped by the sounds of crickets and insects, the scent of flowers, incense, and burning wood.

Before we left for the village, we observed the dog day ritual for the three family dogs, who sat quietly, decorated with marigold necklaces around their necks and tika on their foreheads, waiting patiently for their cookies and milk. We arrived later than expected at the school. Bholla, one of the English teachers, had been there for about 30 minutes, waiting eagerly for us at the gate even though it was a holiday for him. His enthusiasm and anticipation were touching, and indicated how much our visit meant to him.

Our first stop was the village orphanage. Creating an orphanage was Dorje's idea, and all 42 children between the ages of 3 and 15 years were encouraged to attend school. They were thrilled to see us, and welcomed us by blessing us with marigold necklaces and tika (red powder) for our foreheads. Every year since then, we've received the same welcome ritual. Their welcome made it easy for us to jump in and interact with them. Carolyn showed them how to make animals with origami; the others brought soccer balls and kicked them around the playground. I noticed three teenage girls standing shyly against the wall beside the yard and went over to talk to them. It was clear they were eager to practice their English. They asked me how old I was and thought it was really funny that I was 60. We talked about school, and I encouraged them to stay in school for as long as they could so they could find a job. Even though we wanted to stay longer, we left after a short visit, for our second day of interviewing.

Months later, I shared the conversation I had with the girls about staying in school with Rob Moossy, who was the Section Chief of the Criminal Section, Civil Rights Division, US Department of Justice, and worked extensively in human trafficking cases at that time. He urged me not to underestimate the power of my conversation with the girls. He explained that no one had probably ever given this advice to them before. I may have changed their lives, because the message to stay in school given by a Western woman would have a huge impact. This had never occurred to me, because I knew about Oprah's projects in Africa and mine was so small. His comments deepened my appreciation of the impact my groups could have on these children.

When we returned to our cottage, we continued to talk about our experience, compared notes, and stimulated each other's thinking. Our debate continued about whether or not we were imposing our Western values on this village of subsistence farmers, mostly unaffected by Western consumer and cultural values. Beyond what they already have, our interviews indicated their priority is education for their children, for themselves, and a road. Enthusiastically, we carefully entered information on spreadsheets, wrote a summary, and talked for hours exploring what services might be valuable to a village like Dadagaun. Steve and Neeru reassured us that our data would be used for future projects involving other groups. Our experience in the village was a stark contrast to our nonstop, increasingly technologically fractured lives at home.

While we worked on our report, Neeru and her sister prepared a holiday dinner and invited us for informal cooking lessons. We learned how to prepare chicken, dahl (lentil dish), and a chopped vegetable salad using exotic spices like fried fenugreek seed, garlic, ginger, coriander, garum masala, chili powder, paprika, mustard seed, turmeric powder, and mango powder. After our cooking lesson, we enjoyed a relaxing massage given by a masseuse who regularly visited Shivapuri.

Before dinner was served, there was time for a drink on the terrace, watching a movie, and socializing with other guests if we choose to socialize. The night before we left to begin our trek, Steve talked to the group about our travel plans. We only needed clothes for hiking, and incidentals.

Before bed, we sat around the dining room table in our cottage to complete our report and share our ideas about our businesses and our lives. Group members were typically interested in their own inner journeys as well as becoming involved in global issues. Before we left for our trek, we finished our report and emailed it to Steve and Christine, to contribute to the continuity and collaboration in the best interest of the children.

Chapter 14—The Actual Trek

I hardly slept at all the night before we left for the mountains to begin our first trek. We got up at 6 a.m. for an early breakfast and departure. Before we left, I found Neeru to thank her. The first year, I found her sitting on a stool drinking tea in the corner of the small kitchen in our cottage. When I thanked her, with tears in her eyes she said, "Sydney, thank you. You've inspired me. I've wanted to help my own people but didn't know how to do it. Now I know because of you."

En route to the airport, one of the group members exclaimed, "I forgot my passport!" I called Steve who reassured us and urged us to go ahead. After Arjune dropped us off at the airport, we made our way to the gate. It was like a contact sport. We stuck close together through the terminal to our gate to wait for our plane to Pokhara, the bustling adventure travel town built around a lake and the rural capital of Western Nepal. I realized just how privileged we were when my group member without her passport was just waved through check-in. Other than leaving an hour or so late, our 35-minute flight was uneventful. Those who sat on the right side of the plane in rows 11 and 12 had views of the mountains towering above the clouds. After we landed at the small airport, our guide and porters met us and transported us to the travel company's office for a briefing. We sorted our luggage there and just took what we needed in duffel bags. Our drive to the trailhead took about an hour.

Every year, the trek was a little different; but generally, the trail in those early years took us along the ridge line in the lower foothills of the Annapurnas with surrounding views of Pokhara Valley. After about two hours, our route dropped to the Modi River Valley and Gurung Lodge in Majhgaon with a view of Fishtail Mountain. Argune, our guide, took us for an hour hike to a village mid-afternoon, followed by leisure time at the lodge. Tea was served outside our rooms in the late afternoon, with a view of the gardens and the outlines of foothills and mountains covered by clouds. Before we see the mountains, I am often asked if the foothills are the mountains, and people can't believe they aren't since the foothills are larger than most mountains in the States.

After resting, we joined our guides and guests, some involved with global issues and some just traveling for fun. Afterward, we had dinner and went to bed early. In the morning, we woke a little before 6 a.m. and opened our front doors to a spectacular view of the sun hitting Annapurna South. The first person who registered for my first trip was writer, poet and speaker Mozella Perry Ademiluyi. The year she came, I didn't hesitate to knock on her door, knowing she had to see the sun rising over the mountains, not just the foothills. We were like two children filled with excitement, and shared a magnificent awe-inspiring view of Annapurna South. Mozella exclaimed, "Love really is a mountain!" This is the poem she wrote and read to me that morning:

Waking Up To What I Couldn't See
Shrouded… yet in place
not going anywhere
…just waiting for me
Glistening and
spilling truth across
a clear blue sky
Transformed by movement
that lifted just in time
so that when I woke up
The light was on.
…Annapurna smiled[33]

Soon our porter joined us, equally excited by the view. They loved the mountains like members of their family. Each year I returned with a group, and we shared the same wonder and excitement with each

---

[33] Mozella Perry Ademiluyi November, 2011©www.loveisamountain.com

other. I often observed our porters and guides standing quietly, contemplating the mountains. One year I asked about the stories associated with them. The guide I asked looked at me and told me he didn't understand my question. I wondered if there are words in English to describe the animistic legends and nature spirit deities living there for centuries.

We packed our bags before breakfast, giving our porters time to get ready for the day. Our breakfast consisted of cornflakes, hard-boiled eggs, toast, peanut butter, marmalade, potatoes, onions, peppers, sausage, coffee and tea. Our hike started at about 8:30 a.m., through Majhgaunthen, an unspoiled village, the sub-tropical forests containing tree orchids, rhododendrons and magnolias, and past fields of millet, rice, and buckwheat being harvested. Most of the trail is made of grey flat stones used in this region to protect the hillsides from monsoons. We passed through the village of Pothana where many Tibetan traders live and sell their souvenirs. Each day of the hike, we were astounded by the beauty surrounding us. Everywhere we looked, there was a flower we'd never seen before. Ashok, our guide, stopped often to point out a rare bird or orchid. The combination of the visual beauty and the sounds of the birds, insects and animals made us feel like we were in heaven. As one trekker walked along the trail, she looked over at me and exclaimed, "Sydney, my friends will think I photoshopped the pictures of this trek!" Another woman said, "I feel like I am the star in a *National Geographic* show." One of the men said, "Ok, now it's time to extend my visa and become an expat. This is a real reality check. It clarifies what is important."

At night, there was complete darkness and silence, a welcome relief from our hectic noisy lives at home. Here, there was time to contemplate the mountains and reflect on our lives. While hiking, we took frequent breaks to rest and soak in the beauty around us. Some years, Dhaulagiri, the mountain closest to us on the Mustang trek, and the entire Annapurna range were visible in the distance. One of our favorite stops was at Heaven's Gate Café, where we enjoyed sherpa tea—still a favorite of mine — while sitting on the terrace. In subsequent years they would have Wi-Fi, reminding us of how quickly Nepal is changing. As we sipped our tea, we looked over the vast valley as mule trains carrying heavy loads walked past us, their hoofs clinking on the stone path and bells around their necks, chiming softly. Along the way, we often met other trekkers. Once, an American doctor from Denver approached us. She and her husband had just finished two weeks volunteering in a clinic with the Helping Hands.

A few hours after leaving Heaven's Gate, we arrived at the second lodge, Basanta, in time for a late lunch and a panoramic view of the Annapurna Mountain Range. Some years, we were able to see the sweeping view of the entire Annapurna Range, other years the mountains were shrouded in clouds and fog. Lunch was served while we sat on the lawn outside our lodge. Afterward, we could hike to the old village of Shampua with a visit to the museum. At the museum, Ashok delighted in showing us tools and how they were used. The tools are impressive for their efficiency and practicality. After dinner, we fell asleep listening to rain or silence and felt utterly at peace.

On our last day of hiking, we walked along the ridge that descended through wooded hillsides and terraced farmlands to the valley floor where a van waited for us. If there wasn't school, curious children loved to talk with us to practice their English and ask questions about the United States. If there was time, we stopped at a Tibetan refugee camp to visit the monastery and shops selling rugs, art, jewelry, and Buddhist souvenirs.

Our next stop was the trekking company's office in Pokhara for a celebratory farewell ceremony. Back at the office, our porters and guide placed khataks (traditional long white scarves) around our necks to honor and thank us while we sat on white plastic chairs in the garden.

Before our flight, we visited Pokhara for lunch at Kangaroo Cafe on the lake. By this time, we were content to just hang out and didn't mind the slow service. It has surprised me each year to see my companions comfortably let time drift by and joke about being on Nepalese time. Quite an accomplishment for those of us living frantic lifestyles back in the States.

Chapter 15—Farewell Nepal

Sometimes the flight back to Kathmandu was late, but otherwise uneventful. Once we landed in Kathmandu, our next step was to claim our luggage. Carts full of luggage were dumped outside onto a shelf, and everyone, mostly men, pushed ahead of one another to get their luggage. I was relieved to see Neta, a competent young woman Steve hired to meet us. She jumped right into the fray, quickly helped us collect our luggage, and whisked us into the van for a 15-minute drive to Dwarika's Hotel.

This Nepalese-owned hotel is carefully designed and uses traditional Nepalese wood carvings, motifs, and artifacts which make it a work of art, a living museum with purpose. It is an award-winning example of how culture can be preserved through developing a world-class hotel. This stunning design statement is an oasis in the middle of Kathmandu. We were delighted with our rooms and the attentive staff.

After a short rest, we met with Steve, Neeru, and other friends for our farewell dinner in the famous Krishnarpaan restaurant. Often Steve's Nepalese friends joined us, which gave us an opportunity to meet Nepalese professionals. We met fascinating people from near and far, including guests staying at Shivapuri who were interested in hearing about our experiences.

One year, we met a woman from Arizona who had just retrieved her luggage that had been lost for a week and was traveling alone in Nepal and Bhutan for three months. That same year, we met Christine's yoga teacher en route from teaching yoga in India. She had carried Legos to deliver to Dadagaun school. Another year, we met a neuropsychologist working at Mt. Sinai Hospital in New York City who raised money from her "Sweet Dreams" project to contribute new mattresses, sheets, and teddy bears to replace the urine-soaked, bedbug-infested ones in the orphanage in Dadaguan Village.

Meeting other people who contribute to the greater good in the world enriched our cultural experience as we sat comfortably on big pillows on the floor around a low rectangular-shaped table. We enjoyed learning about each other while eating a festive multi-course dinner traditionally served during Nepalese religious ceremonies. The meal began with an assortment of hors d'oeuvres, like buckwheat pancakes with chickpeas and lentils. The next courses included momos, mixed vegetable soups, rice, chicken curry, stir-fried potato and cauliflower, sautéed mixed organic spinach, homemade pickles, and finally fruit salad with spiced yogurt.

After dinner, it was time to say goodbye to Steve and Neeru. It was especially sad for me to say goodbye to Neeru. Each year, our friendship and respect for each other have deepened. Her comments, given to me privately, gave me ideas for future projects that inevitably result in a memorable experience for our group members and make everlasting contributions to the lives we touch.

Since most of the flights back to the United States leave at night there was one more day to spend in Kathmandu. If Steve had time, he joined us to take us on a walk through the parts of Thamel that tourists don't frequent. One year, we bought spices, tea, and jewelry made from glass beads to take home with us. In other years, I arranged another tour. One of our favorite places to visit was the Nepali Folk Musical Instrument Museum (https://musicmuseumnepal.org/). Some group members simply rested and enjoyed the hotel.

Before leaving that first year, Steve and I met to debrief. After our first Trek of Your Life trip in 2011, we happily agreed our experiment was highly successful and planned our next voluntourism trip. For many years, Steve and Sohan enthusiastically inspired me to bring another group to Nepal.

Chapter 16—Meeting with Christine and Kurt on Skype

The first successful TOYL trip gave me the impetus to continue my journey. Carolyn Buppert, a member of the first group, bought several books on service projects in Nepal when she got home. She gave them to me. My favorite was *Bringing Progress to Paradise* by Jeff Rasley. I wrote to him to ask for a consultation. He wrote back and asked me if I'd like to be on the Basa Foundation Board. I was hesitant and asked if I could visit the village before I decided. Jeff introduced me to Niru Rai, the founder of GeoTrek. Niru and I met for the first time in 2012. Since that meeting, we have worked together.

I invited the group that had been on the trek and people who were interested in joining for a Nepalese dinner at my home. Guests enjoyed food made from Neeru's recipes and a Skype session with Christine. After dinner and lively, enthusiastic conversation, we finally met Christine via Skype. Now that our paths had crossed from opposite corners of the world, I was curious to learn more about Christine and Kurt's journey. Christine told her story. She visited the Dadagaun Village school as a volunteer teaching English for one month in 2007. Her sincerity and enthusiasm were palpable. This was the beginning of our collaboration working together on behalf of Dadagaun Village for many years.

Later, I learned more about Christine. She was a speech therapist and mother of three who had sadly divorced after a long marriage. She saw this time in her life as a transition and began planning a three-month trip to Nepal to trek, breathe the mountain air, get to know Nepalese people, and volunteer as an English teacher. Needing "to get fit," as she said, she joined the Brisbane Bushwalker's Club. On her first hike, she met Kurt, a widower and father of two married sons. His love of the outdoors, nature, and people drew him to the same walking club where he met Christine. When he learned of Christine's plans to go to Nepal for three months, he asked if he could join her for part of the time. She invited him to join her for one month.

Six weeks after they met, they were trekking in Nepal. Kurt asked Christine to marry him under prayer flags on Renjo La Pass in the Everest Region. She accepted. While in Nepal, Christine's interest in teaching English took her to Dadaguan Village School. Needing a place to stay near the school, Christine found Shivapuri Cottage and met the Websters. Steve and Neeru began collaborating with the Marschners, and have continued to play a crucial role in monitoring and sustaining the projects related to Dadagaun Village. For nearly ten years, Kurt and Christine continued to share their love of Nepal, and we worked together on the Dadaguan Village Project. They raised funds to supplement and train the teachers, coordinated scholarship programs to pay tuition for high school students, and spent time there working with the principal and staff. Christine told me that when she started working with the teachers, she found beautiful children's books safely locked in a closet getting moldy. The staff were afraid to use them and didn't know how. Each year I've visited there since, the progress continued. When I visited the school after the pandemic in 2022, I was delighted to see the new preschool building and the same teachers using updated programs.

With Steve and Neeru's help, other volunteers, like my groups, have become involved and enjoy visiting Dadagaun village to volunteer. During the last 14 years, TOYL groups have provided scholarships for children to attend high school, created a dance/music program, recorded social histories for the orphans, paid school fees, and taught the teachers and teen-age girls how to sew washable sanitary napkins so they could attend classes during their periods, taught parenting classes, created and maintained their first computer room, taught and participated in other classes, donated school supplies, and purchased a new printer.

After the computer room was established, Dhorje told me village mothers were learning how to use computers at night. Gradually, they decided to organize a mothers' group, and in 2015 asked to meet with me for encouragement and coaching. They didn't need much! In a few years, they opened a bank account, and are now selling organic fruit, vegetables, and flowers at local markets. In 2018, with Neeru's help, they learned how to make organic compost to sell, too. When we visited in 2022, I learned they were also performing cultural dances and playing music in the hotels that have sprung up around Dadagaun Village. In 2023 I sent $500.00 dollars donated to me to purchase a sound system for them. The progress is undeniable and overwhelmingly rewarding. As one group member said, "A little donation goes a long way in Nepal."

Chapter 17—What We Do

Thanks to Skype and the internet, Steve, Neeru and I have collaborated with Dhorje, the teachers, Christine, and Kurt to make sure we are true to our mission and coordinate our efforts. Each service project led to another. Niru Rai met with me while I was in Kathmandu in 2012. When we met, he and I made plans for me to trek to Basa Village in 2013. At that time, Basa wasn't even on a map, it was that remote.

In the second year (2012), there were three group members, Audrey and Barry Suskind and Brian King. Brian signed up in August because another trip he was interested in didn't have enough people. If he hadn't joined us, I might have given up the idea of taking groups to Nepal. Brian asked me before we left if we could use a laptop for the school. After checking with Steve and Christine, we each added a donated laptop to our luggage. When Steve learned that we were donating laptops, he used a $3,000 donation from a school in Doha to install solar panels as backup electricity. Christine remembered that

Mozella had offered to make a donation and contacted her to give money for the computer room. All Mozella asked in return was for me to give two Wayne Dyer books to a young man she had met the year before.

When Barry arrived at the school, he and Brian went to work immediately to wire the computers and orient the teachers and students. The computers were a surprise for them. They could hardly believe they were getting computers and access to the internet. Brian told me it took just minutes for them to learn. Barry lit up like a kid in a candy shop with excitement and worked patiently on the technical aspects with Dorje. His wife, Audrey, an accountant, taught Dorje how to use an Excel sheet to track his expenses and email the spreadsheet to Christine in Australia. After we made sure the others were busy, Neeru and I facilitated a moms' parenting group, using concepts and a video I had from a Train the Trainer CEFEL program I took before I left my county job (http://csefel.vanderbilt.edu/). Neeru put the ideas into context for the moms, and they were laughing and enjoying our time together within 10 minutes.

After the staff thanked us for our service by giving us certificates and necklaces made from marigolds, Barry looked at me and said, "I've never done anything like this before. I just changed the lives of 60 people." Barry continues to clean and configure donated laptops for various TOYL projects. Since then, we've contributed a total of about 40 laptops, approximately 165 hours on-site, and approximately 20 hours of technical support via Skype. We've collected toothbrushes, combs, balls, pencils, paper, educational games, posters, and books to be used in classrooms. Last year, Steve told our group that we had spent more time with the children in the orphanage than anyone else involved. It is our time and interest in their village that is valued more than the material gifts we give them. For them, practicing English with native speakers is priceless.

In 2013, we trekked to Basa Village. I met Buddhi Rai (the lead guide, Siddhar) and Ram Rai, the cook. We've worked together happily for years since then. This trek was cut short because the Phaplu Airport, closest to Basa, was closed. Ten of us rode in two four-wheel drive vehicles for a memorably uncomfortable 18-hour drive over fiercely rugged terrain. Two women, over 50 years old, sat strapped in together in the front seat and talked happily with each other the whole way. The car ride delayed our arrival to Basa by two days, and we didn't have time to stop and visit Tibetan monasteries in the region. Yet one goes with the flow when in Nepal. Expecting the unexpected and adjusting the course were skills I learned on that trek.

After the trek, we returned to Shivapuri to rest and volunteer. Neeru provided a simple form for us to complete, and arranged for us to interview children in the orphanage who previously had no records. We sat on well-worn wooden benches by a makeshift table in the children's home yard for the interviews. The teenagers were eager to practice English, and carefully helped us spell names correctly and encouraged the younger ones to participate. While we completed the forms, Neeru took individual photos of each child to attach to the completed forms and created a file for each child.

When I asked how they felt about living in the orphanage, all but one said, "Very happy." We learned that many of them had been abandoned and lost until Ramesh (the "orphanage father") came to get them or someone from their village took them to the children's home. The little girl who was sad to be there responded to my questions about her village and parents. I used this informal opportunity to model for Ramesh, who was sitting with me, how important it is to encourage her to talk about her feelings, to help her adjust.

With Neeru's help, we collaborated with their "parents," Ramesh (father) and Gita (mother), who requested we talk with the children about washing their hands, picking up trash, and brushing their teeth. Neeru provided laminated drawings of trash, handwashing, and toothbrushing for us to use to encourage the children to make a habit of these things. Before we started, they sat respectfully on a big tarp in the courtyard while we explained the importance of respecting ourselves, each other, and their home. With our help, the children enthusiastically posted the signs around their home. They delighted in finding places to hang the signs and place the recycling baskets. One rainy afternoon, we encouraged them to draw pictures with the paper, crayons, and markers we brought with us. Afterward, without fanfare, Neeru framed some of the drawings to hang on the walls of the children's home, which were previously bare.

Steve and Neeru carefully monitored our activities and donations and taught me to be more sensitive to Nepalese culture. For instance, Steve explained that he'd keep the 60 toothbrushes we brought with us in 2012 until a rack was built to keep them and names were written on each toothbrush. One by one, he planned to trade the old one for a new one. After our trek, when we returned to see the children again, the new mattresses and bedding had been delivered and installed. I happened to observe Neeru showing Gita and the older girls how to make a corner while making a bed. How else would they learn these skills that may lead to jobs in hotels in the future? As we were leaving that day, one of the teachers in my group said, "Sydney, these children are HAPPY! And they have nothing."

Before leaving, Neeru mentioned it would be nice to help the women in the village learn a craft to produce a product, an item they could sell to earn a little pocket money for themselves. Two ideas were jam from the plums, which are abundant and used to make raksi, a kind of whiskey, and jewelry.

Chapter 18—The Trek Continues

Each year, I questioned and reexamined my mission, which involved deep introspection and collaborating with my advisors Rich, Pauline, Carolyn, Mozella, Audrey, Barry, and other group members. They have become friends and support my business in ways I never expected.

One of the most generous supporters is Jim Forman. As a volunteer, I got to know Jim, in his role of Conference and Volunteer Mastermind, at the Psychotherapy Networker Conference with 3,000 participants and 200 volunteers. He learned of my interest in Nepal, wondered if I was familiar with a school he learned about, and the rest is a beautiful, ongoing relationship with TOYL. Yearly, since 2014, Jim has donated increasingly generous amounts to the school. His devoted generosity turned to love when he received the Facebook video created by the students to thank him. During the pandemic, he stepped up to donate hundreds of dollars monthly for food, scholarships, and computers. Their correspondence continues. During one of many phone calls with Jim, he said, "I love donating to them. It gives me such joy and satisfaction to know that I can make such a difference in so many lives. We have so much, and citizens in other parts of the world have so very little... I count my blessings each and every day. Let me know what you need, or how I can help the kids... thanks so much for introducing me to this amazing group of Nepalese adults and children."

Encouragement and new ideas come at the most unexpected times. For instance, one day while I was standing in my kitchen washing dishes and listening to the radio, I heard an interview with Paul Hawken about his book, *Blessed Unrest*. He explained that because of the internet, small groups were working with each other to solve problems without government support.

The New York Times summarized: "The movement, as Paul Hawken calls it, is made up of an unknowable number of citizens and mostly ragtag organizations that come and go. But when you do see it, you understand it to include NGOs, nonprofit agencies, and a seemingly disparate range of people who might describe themselves as environmental activists, as well as people who might not describe themselves as anything at all but are protesting labor injustices, monitoring estuaries, supporting local farming or defending native people from being robbed of the last forests. There are a few billionaires, working hard to give their wealth away, and there are even some Christian evangelicals, who have decided the earth is not theirs to trash, but the movement is mostly about shared beliefs, even if those beliefs are unproclaimed."[34]

After reading his book, I realized that our work on behalf of Dadagaun Village is a small part of this global movement. This premise gave me a great deal of comfort for the future of our world.

One step kept leading to another. I organized two fundraisers in a nearby Nepalese restaurant in my neighborhood. These events proved to be a great way to introduce previous group members to people interested in our project and raise money for school supplies. The owner invited the Nepalese Ambassador to the first event, and Tara Linhardt, co-founder of the Mountain Music Project, agreed to join us for the second one.

It was serendipitous how Tara and I met. After a Synergy Dance class, a musician in the class said, "Sydney, you need to meet Tara Linhardt." Tara had performed, lectured, and led discussions about Nepali culture and music at National Geographic in Washington D.C., the Rubin Museum in New York City, American University, the Smithsonian Folklife Festival, and the Asia Society, just to name a few. She has lived and studied in Nepal for long periods of time and is fluent in the language, as well as having a

---

[34] The New York Times, Book Review, August 5, 2007,

thorough understanding of the culture and how to explain aspects of that culture to a Western audience.

When I started to plan the October 2014 trip, I thought of Tara when I remembered the children in the orphanage were performing Justin Bieber dances and songs with one drum for accompaniment. I asked Tara to join us. She was key to creating the music program, and we had a fundraiser at Sarangi, a restaurant managed by musicians. She explained that when international travelers visit villages like Dadagaun, indigenous people learn that their knowledge, music, dance and art developed through centuries have value. After talking with her, I launched a CrowdRise campaign to raise money to help enhance the school curriculum, improve academic success and attendance by hiring a music teacher to teach at the school. We were able to buy sarangis (fiddles), bansuris (flutes), and madals (drums). Who knows? With practice, the children may be able to perform and have careers performing and teaching music.

While consulting with Christine before I left, she explained that if the children in the orphanage could pay their school fees ($52 per year) the school could be self-sustaining. By the time I left for Nepal, $1,600 more was donated and I deposited the money directly into the school's bank account for the orphans' fees. When I visited the school the next year, Dhorje, the principal, said, "The music program has changed the minds of the students. They ask when their music class will be. They are so sad if they miss a class, and they practice in their free time. The parents also think their children are creating new things. I would like it to continue."

Chapter 19—Resilient Hearts: Trekking in Nepal after the Earthquake

Frankly, it felt too risky to take another group to Nepal in 2015. The 7.6 magnitude earthquake that hit on April 25, 2015, and its continuing aftershocks for many months, meant traveling there would be riskier than other years. The Gorkha earthquake's epicenter was about 76 kilometers northwest of the capital, Kathmandu. It was followed by more than 300 aftershocks. Around 9,000 people were killed, of whom approximately 55 percent were female, and over 100,000 people were injured. The upheaval was political, as well, with unrest erupting into protests against a new constitution. Consequently, the border between India and Nepal was blocked, making resources—especially fuel—scarce.

I was heartbroken and torn about whether to go personally, let alone take a trekking group with me. I kept thinking about the people, like the young mother I talked with in 2011, who would do anything to educate herself and her daughter. In my many trips to Nepal, I have faced the unknown repeatedly, from unexpected changes in our itinerary to closed airports due to damaged runways from heavy rain. But nothing like this. The country was shattered. After a flurry of emails, my contacts and friends in Nepal gave me the go-ahead in late July. I decided to take a chance. But just in case something happened to me, I sent copies of my travel insurance to each of my adult children.

Even before the earthquake, I felt stalled, and had just three people registered for the trek. I contacted Jeff Rasley, and we agreed I'd join his group instead. But more people were to join us because of a seemingly unrelated event I had organized in January. I took a few hikers with me to meet Paul Kiczek, the founder of Free Walkers, who had organized a 26-mile hike on the canal to commemorate Robert Kennedy's walk on the canal in 1963. We planned to say hello, walk a few miles and go out to lunch. When I met Paul, I handed him a TOYL flyer. It never crossed my mind that he would partner with me in the future.

Once I made my decision, I checked with Jeff Rasley about his trip, which I learned he had canceled. It seemed to me that of all years to trek in Nepal, this trip would be important. So for the first time, I worked directly with GeoTrek, which cut the trip cost in half because the middleman was eliminated.

I contacted Paul to see if he knew anyone who'd like to join the trek. He offered to send out an email blast on the Free Walkers list serve. He attracted more hikers even though he couldn't endorse TOYL. In the following years, he and I gave talks together at REI in NYC and NJ about FreeWalkers and TOYL. Word spread that the trip was on, and nine self-reliant trekkers registered for the 2015 trek. Niru Rai created an itinerary for my group that would require a moderate skill-level trek to his tiny home village located in the Solukhumbu District, south of Everest. Basa was so remote, it couldn't be found on a map or Google Earth. This is why I wanted to return. The untouched beauty of the region and the villagers' kindness, resilience, and uncomplaining ability to adapt to a tough environment left me yearning to go back.

Yet one goes with the flow when in Nepal. To expect the unexpected and adjust the course were skills I had learned from my previous adventures, and I knew they would define my post-earthquake trip. My goal for this trip was to spend more time in the village and complete a survey about what the villagers needed most. And on a personal level, I longed to re-experience crossing a 10,000-foot pass with views of Everest and surrounding snow-capped giants.

When I arrived in Kathmandu that year, an associate looked into my eyes and said, "The true friends of Nepal are coming this year." My trepidations began to fall away. It felt good to be back.

In spite of the scarcity of fuel, Niru had everything moving smoothly. Man Bir, Niru's assistant, and the driver met each travel-wearied group member by placing marigold garlands around their necks and said, "Namaste" upon arrival. Each of us was transported by van to our hotel without a hitch. As we passed fuel lines several miles long, I asked Niru, "How on earth are you managing your business with the fuel crisis?" "We've stockpiled fuel," he said. "We have to because these things happen." Niru went on explain that a cousin who lived near the border was getting fuel for him.

In previous years, it seemed nearly impossible to cross the narrow, chaotic streets and breathe the thick polluted air in Kathmandu. I'd become somewhat accustomed to the honking cars, wandering cows, rickshaws, overloaded buses, vendors, rackety motorcycles, the visual cacophony of hopelessly tangled electrical and phone wires, and dazzling bursts of blues, yellows, and oranges of the flowers and the women's saris. This year, we strolled through relatively quiet streets, watching for bicycles and the occasional taxi or motorcycle.

As we visited the first World Heritage site in Kathmandu on our tour, Durbar Square, my heart dropped at the contrast with my prior visits. Those of us who'd been there before had mixed feelings as we gazed at crumbling walls, stacks of bricks beside the shrines, and long poles supporting fragile walls. We grieved the architectural damage and cultural loss, yet there was still that magical something, as always.

Murmuring practitioners chanted their mantras and performed spiritual rituals, and smoky trails of burning incense scented the air with juniper berry and other spices. Tables covered with butter lamps flickered with a warm glow; and as always, there were bright orange marigold garlands for sale near the temples and stupas that were being rebuilt.

In spite of Niru's reassurance, I was apprehensive about trekking to Basa Village. I had read that landslides had wiped out some trails, and I worried about earthquake damage. Once we left our home base in Kathmandu, we entered another world, one unseen by most Americans. Three guides, a cook, and 21 porters and assistants were our support team. All 25 of them were from Basa Village. They were clearly excited that we were going to visit their home and, not incidentally, it was a chance to show off their success to friends and families.

My concerns about the challenges were largely unfounded. We hiked unimpeded through tranquil rainforests and past small Tibetan villages towards Basa. As we drew near, five musicians playing horns and beating drums escorted us down the path into the schoolyard. Ursula, a Basa Village Foundation board member who'd trekked to Basa in 2009, traded wondrous looks with me, and we looked forward to the welcome we'd share with others. Children waited with marigold garlands to place around each of our necks. I had so many stacked around my neck that I could barely see over them. I put the rest on my arm and gratefully sat on benches in the schoolyard for a welcoming ceremony, surrounded by smiling faces. One of my oldest group members said, "I've never felt so much love."

Pauline, veteran traveler, climber, and my tent mate for the exploratory trek to Mustang in 2010, rose to place some of her garlands around the necks of the smaller bright-eyed children sitting nearby; they were delighted. In the following days, the villagers welcomed us into their homes by serving fresh buffalo milk, local whiskey, quinces and cucumbers. Their homes were surrounded by a riot of flowers— chrysanthemums, roses, red bougainvillea. We saw a bounty of color and food you don't often see in the average American backyard.

As we visited each home, Buddhi, our guide and interpreter, assisted me in completing the surveys. Each villager we talked with expressed gratitude for the electricity, water, and smokeless stoves that were purchased with money raised in the States. They no longer had to carry water for one or two hours a day from the river below. With the offer of funds for materials, the villagers took the initiative to plan and execute these projects. They wanted to ease hardship, provide opportunities for their children, improve health, and prevent unnecessary death. Over the years, my appreciation for their endurance, resourcefulness, and cooperative work style has deepened. Their culture is rooted in ancient secular values that foster peaceful living, interconnectedness, and respect for spirit in things, animals and people.

One of our group members, a retired teacher, led the children in lively activities to practice their English. Others of us counted in English as we tossed cheery marigold blossoms back and forth with them. Over and over, villagers took our hands, looked into our eyes, and said, "You are in our family. We wish we could tell you what is in our hearts."

Before dinner, the night before we left to continue our trek, Mo's (Pauline's common-law husband) back became so painful he couldn't even roll over in his sleeping bag. Coincidently, the shaman performed a ceremony that night. Afterward, he went into Mo's tent with incense and other tools. The next morning, Mo was able to start trekking again. We'll never know what helped him. Another trekker had given him muscle relaxers, I worked with Mo giving him some polarity contacts for his back, or/and the shaman's work. It seemed like a miracle had occurred.

The village shaman and other members of the leadership team explained the nearest medical clinic was an hour and a half away and often without medicine. Mo, whose son was in nursing school in Massachusetts, asked, "How much does it cost to send someone to nursing school?"

Buddhi explained it cost $15,000 for two years, an almost unimaginable amount for these people. Later on the trail, Mo said, "Sydney, I'll pay for the costs of nursing school. Be sure to get in touch with me about it. No wonder people from all over the world who come here want to set up hospitals and schools. They captured my heart."

When it was time to leave the village and continue our trek, the respected elder said, "We don't know why you come." I watched his patient, lined face as our translator spoke to me. I replied, "Because you have things we don't have in the United States. It feels good to be here with you."

As we walked out of the schoolyard, women and children placed marigold garlands around our necks as a final gesture of friendship. The band and several of the children escorted us as we started up the trail. During a rest stop, Pauline looked at me with tears in her eyes. "Sydney, nowhere else in the world is there such genuine helpfulness and kind generosity. This is why I keep coming back to Nepal."

We continued our trek on well-worn paths, ascending, descending, crossing rivers, and walking through forests and tiny Tibetan villages. Most seemed to have stayed largely intact despite the earthquake's best efforts to shake them off their cliffside perches. As we made our slow way to Lukla, where we'd end our trek, we stopped to see Buddhist temples perfumed by centuries of incense, one containing fragile scrolls hundreds of years old. We camped in fragrant orange and lemon groves, in a grassy field with water buffaloes nearby, on banks near the river, and in first-class camping sites with spectacular views of the mountains. We delighted in sharing warming mugs of masala tea (black tea with ginger, cardamom, milk and sugar) while we rested in various teashops along the way. Each time I reintroduced myself to a Tibetan tea shop owner or a sherpa whom I'd met in 2013, he hugged me while telling me, "We had a bad year." Such an understatement. I'm sure they were especially pleased to see us as a sign that the tourist industry was returning. Since they speak just a few words in English and I don't speak Nepalese, we relied on our eye contact and physical connection to convey appreciation and compassion for what they'd experienced.

The only other groups we saw were service groups. A tall, lanky British man on the trail stopped to talk with me. He said, "The only groups here this year are volunteering." When I asked him what he was doing he said, "I work for a project writing the history of this region by interviewing the Sherpas." I was enthralled by meeting people like him.

Mid-day on our seventh day, we reached the pass. Sitting by myself, I brushed tears away as I gazed across deeply forested valleys to 15 of the largest jagged, snow-capped giants surrounding

Everest. I felt uplifted and appreciated the wonder of being a part of the beauty around me. My soul swelled as I thought of the infinite possibilities we have. I treasured these rare moments of complete peace and serenity. This is one of the memories I took with me as a sort of spiritual talisman when I returned to the States.

That year, as with every year I've taken a group to Nepal, we had an experience that far exceeded my vision. The earthquake tested the Nepalese's resilience and spirit. It is a long road back, but they are determined. As I flew back to Washington, D.C., I thought back to the children's expectant faces as we created their computer lab, the dancing and singing at the Kathmandu fundraising concert, the sherpas who guided me, and the sewing machine for the mother seeking the respectable future of a tailor. These are friends who live on the other side of the world and yet, at the same time, live in my heart. I'm inspired by all the small yet impactful ways a small group of people contributed to the global movement for peace and security.

Chapter 20—Another Step into the Human Trafficking World

After my first trip to Nepal, I focused on time-consuming administrative tasks like creating a flyer, applying for a trademark, hiring a neighbor to rewrite the necessary forms for trip registration, and speaking to groups about the trek. With a majority of these tasks underway, one sunny brisk morning on my way to my office, elated and carrying the brand-new box of flyers, I stopped to say hello to an acquaintance sitting on a bench outside in the sun. As we chatted about my first trip to Nepal, a man sitting next to him turned to me and said, "My wife's daughter just got back from Nepal and worked in human trafficking for five years," and offered to give me her contact information. She was easy to find, because her mother is a social worker and had an office across the hall from mine.

A few weeks later, the three of us met for a conversation to discuss human trafficking. When I asked my colleague's daughter, "What could someone with my skills possibly do to contribute to healing victims?" She said, "Most of the staff working in these programs were victims themselves. They need training on self-care and basic counseling skills." I loved the idea but had no idea how to proceed.

A few weeks after that, I read a notice on the clinical society list-serve about a series of trainings on issues related to human trafficking. The workshops were offered gratis in 2013 by the Intercultural Counseling Connection, Loyola University Counseling Center, and the Baltimore Maryland Chapter of the National Association of Social Workers. In exchange, we were asked to provide pro bono counseling for refugees. For seven years, I provided pro bono counseling for refugees from Eritrea, Sudan, Iraq, and Burundi. The interpreters who worked with me were from Egypt, Ruanda, and Sudan. It was a deeply rewarding experience.

During one of the workshops, I met Bharati Devkota, a Nepalese counselor and Ayurvedic doctor who moved her family to the States because her husband worked at Johns Hopkins. During a break, I introduced myself and shared my idea to give workshops to staff members rescuing survivors of trafficking in Nepal. Bharati's eyes filled with tears. She loved the idea and wanted to work with me.

After I completed the program, I felt I had an entree to email Shannon, the contact given to me two years ago at Shivapuri Cottage. She graciously introduced me to several groups rescuing and rehabilitating trafficked women and children in Nepal. Before returning to Kathmandu in 2013, I planned meetings with them in Nepal. Since there were two TOYL groups scheduled in addition to Annapurna, I trekked to Basa Village. I had plenty of time to meet with Shannon's contacts.

My first meeting was with Dhru Thapa, founder of the New Hope Foundation. He told me that when he was a little boy, his father left Nepal, not to return for years. Dhru and his family survived on what money he and his mother could make. Eventually, he worked as a houseboy for a family in Kathmandu and got an education. His father eventually returned home, which marked the family's descent into the world of HIV-AIDS in a very personal way.

A young man by then, Dhru vowed that he would do all he could to help the women and their children who had fallen victim to human trafficking and subsequently taken their place in a new "untouchable" caste—to be shunned for the rest of their lives because they had contracted HIV-AIDS. Since then, Dhru has assembled a heroic team that works tirelessly to run a hospice for these victims. Before he left our meeting, he invited me to visit the hospice and to have lunch in his home, where he and his wife take care of about 30 children whose parents have abandoned them or whose parents have AIDS, and in some cases both. I hoped I could accept his invitation after my first group left and before my next group arrived.

Two weeks later, Glenda Houser, the program manager for Beauty for Ashes International (www.beautyforashesintl.com), met me at Dwarika's Hotel. We took a cab to her apartment across town, near Patan. After a stop in her apartment, I rode on the back of her motorcycle to see her program, which was housed in a large mansion enclosed by a garden wall. They make products that reflect Nepalese culture by incorporating as many materials as possible found locally. Just like their name, they love taking things that others would consider worthless and creating something beautiful.

Since it was a holiday, none of the artisans who make and sell jewelry, infinity scarves and small bags using recycled cloth from saris were there. As we walked from room to room, she explained that she first came to Nepal with a Christian group to rescue survivors, because she felt like there was something missing from her life as a successful stockbroker in Florida. Originally, she planned to stay for six months. She stayed for eight years. She told me that once a person is rescued, she lives in a safe house until she can find a job and support herself. Unfortunately, many are not able to leave, and risk being resold because they don't have jobs.

Glenda's program teaches tailoring and jewelry making to these women, allowing them to save money and get their own apartments. The program benefits from the expertise of a number of volunteers. One of these is a jewelry maker from New York City who taught jewelry design and continues to give advice via Skype. Glenda was pleased to accept the laptop I had brought to donate. I loved the designs and bought several gifts to take home, and decided to add a stop there to the itinerary.

Afterward, I rode on the back of Glenda's motorcycle to meet Dhru at a nearby corner, then rode on the back of his motorcycle to the hospice and New Hope's workshop. (My father would have killed me if he'd known I was riding on the back of motorcycles in Kathmandu traffic.) While we were there, he gave me two small bracelets with "I gave hope" carved on a piece of silver with woven strings to make the band. After I returned to the States, I sold these bracelets to raise money for New Hope.

Next, we rode to his home for lunch. The large, peaceful, spacious house, sparsely furnished, was surrounded by gardens and a garden wall. While we talked about the needs of his program, his wife served me a traditional Nepalese meal of rice, dahl and greens. His plan was to buy property in the foothills, build a place for the women and children to live, apartments for volunteers, and grow coffee to be sustainable. In subsequent years, he achieved his goals. In 2016, Dhru picked four trekkers up at our hotel to tour his facility. In addition to housing for the women and children, there was housing for volunteers, gardens, and breathtaking views of the mountains. One trekker donated 40 school uniforms she had carried all the way from Austin, Texas.

A few days before I returned to the United States, I received a lovely email from Shakti Samuha requesting a meeting. Since time was short, we had the meeting at a cafe near Boudhanath the day I was leaving Kathmandu. During our brief meeting, the founder, the program manager, and one of the counselors expressed interest in my proposal to provide a workshop to help staff cope with the pressure and stress inherent in their jobs. During that meeting, they explained other groups came to help them, but didn't return and used photographs to promote their own businesses. I understood it would take a while to build trust.

During the following year, I followed up and emailed them repeatedly, but didn't get a reply. I was beginning to think they didn't want me to give a workshop, when it occurred to me to check with Shannon, who'd given me the contact. She asked, "Did I give you contact information for Indira?" No, she hadn't.

Indira responded immediately by email, we talked on the telephone before I left for Nepal, and we met for coffee at Dwarika's Hotel on a free day in the morning. Indira is the founder of Change Action Nepal (www.changeactionnepal.org). When she was a young adult, she was identified as an emerging leader in Nepal by a foundation in the United States. She received training in the United States until the foundation lost its funding. While we sat on the terrace, she explained that sometimes Nepalese are embarrassed about their English and won't reply to emails. This had never occurred to me. She reassured me by offering to make arrangements for the training.

My cousin Gwen had joined the group that year and agreed to spend a few extra days in Kathmandu. I welcomed her company and support. After leaving Shivapuri Cottage, we had a ride to the other side of Kathmandu where expats and international projects are located. Our contact, Kiran, met us on a corner and led us through an alley to our apartment. I could hardly breathe, I was so nervous. As Gwen reached for the brass knob on the blue-painted wooden front door, she exclaimed, "This is just like Paris!" Her confidence put me at ease immediately.

I was apprehensive about my meeting at Shakti Samuha, finding it, getting there through Kathmandu traffic, and being on time. I had no idea how it would go. Niru, who took us on the Basa Village trek, had offered to drive me there. Not only did he find us, he found Shakti Samuha's office, and took us to a tiny cafe to buy tea because we were early for the meeting.

When the meeting started, it was a nice surprise that one of the co-founders, Charimaya Tamang, joined us with three other staff members. Charimaya speaks little English, and I speak less Nepalese. Nevertheless, we feel a strong connection with each other. After one of our workshops in 2016, we just held hands and cried together. In addition to encouraging me, Gwen took pictures of our first meeting.

One English-speaking staff member explained that most staff members had been trafficked themselves and needed help with their own stress-induced physical symptoms. They also needed to learn how to take care of themselves, and how to listen in a way that helps them cope with what they hear from others. They explained their hesitancy in working with foreigners: sometimes groups approach them to teach hair styling or other skills and use the experience to promote themselves, instead of following up with the women they trained. Since that meeting, we emailed regularly and I talked with Bharati, who met with Shakti Samuha when she visited her family in Nepal that year. We planned to give the two-day training they requested in October 2015. If our workshop was successful, we hoped to train others to give it in other parts of the world. Little did I know at that time that on April 25, 2015 there would be an earthquake that would devastate Nepal.

After my meeting with Indira, Dhru met me for coffee because I'd written him to ask if he'd like one of the laptops I'd carried with me. During our coffee, he told me that his group had sold enough $5 bracelets to raise $5,000 to use as a deposit for some land. He'd mentioned this dream to me the year before, and when I heard how much progress he'd made, I called several group members who'd mentioned they'd like to meet him. That afternoon, Dhru explained that once the land is purchased, a Swiss non-governmental organization will donate coffee plants, equipment, and training. If what he's pulled off in the past 20 years is any indication, his vision of establishing a small coffee plantation on the hospice site and growing other produce while the coffee trees are maturing came true. The coffee business helped make the hospice a sustainable effort.

His sincerity, clarity, determination, and intention about his calling moved my cousin from North Carolina to volunteer to sell some of the bracelets the hospice women and children had crafted. My sister from Austin, Texas, and some other tour buddies jumped in and offered to do the same. In fact, one said, "Let's have an event to sell them for Christmas presents."

Back in Maryland, Lauren and Mal Stempler hosted and planned the fund-raiser after we returned. They bought Nepalese food to serve and generated a festive atmosphere. Lauren and I knew each other from Synergy Dance and Polarity Therapy Trainings. I had no idea at that time that she and Mal would continue to produce videos and support trainings we gave in Nepal. About 40 people attended the party, and we raised a total of $3,000 for New Hope Foundation. It was a privilege to witness this unexpected, moving personal transformation. These open-minded group members changed their priorities, increased their capacity for relating to others, and contributed to something bigger than themselves.

CONCLUSION

My first trip to Nepal in 2000 changed the trajectory of my life. Over the past 15 years, I've trekked in Upper Mustang, the Everest region, the Annapurna Range Circuit (five times), Langtang (twice), Basa Village (three times), and Tsum Valley in Nepal, Bhutan, and Tibet. In Nepal, I've worked in two villages, Dadagaun and Basa, as part of service projects sponsored by existing groups with continuing commitments to these villages.

The trek to Tsum Valley in 2022 was challenging for my group of 10. Many were repeat trekkers and their friends. In spite of walking on roads and across unexpected landslides, each member maintained a positive attitude, and good spirits, and went with the flow. While I was training for the trek, I noticed that I didn't seem to be getting stronger. Long story short, I needed a great deal of support on the trek and was diagnosed with ALS when I returned to the States.

Everything changed at once after my diagnosis. I closed my practice and moved back to D.C. from Hudson Valley, New York to have the option to end my life. I'm devastated, of course, but grateful I've been able to contribute to making our world a better one. I'm heartened that Debra Chang, who was in the Tsum Valley group, has agreed to take my role leading the moderate-level trek in Annapurna in 2024. I hope to return to Nepal with the group, but the sad aspect of ALS is that there isn't a timeline and the path is clear.

I've taken over 120 people to Nepal. Group members witnessed how a clean mattress, playing a game, reading, or music lessons on a traditional flute can change a child's life. The surprise for many who join is not only the personal connection they make with villagers but also their new connection with themselves.

My spirit was touched, my mind expanded, my heart opened, and I had a long look at my limiting beliefs. Before my first trip, I felt breathless, as if I was running through life, juggling the demands of work, family, and friends. Our culture of stressing productivity, material wealth, and using people instead of loving people had a deadening effect on me. I didn't want to end up like others, living a life of regret like my father, dead at sixty-two years. Unconsciously, I yearned to escape these negative aspects of our culture and give myself time to observe, reflect and question whether we really need to acquire all those things and do all those things we feel we ought to get done, or rather to connect with others, and myself.

People who have joined my socially conscious trips to Nepal told me the experience was "healing," it "restored my soul," "reminded me about what is important in life," "Layers of armor I didn't know I had, just rolled off me," "Being in that kind of nature is primal and restorative in a way I never experienced before," "Something got under my skin there, I'll never forget it," and "I've traveled to so many places but never experienced the connection to other group members or the country as I did on this trip."

Inevitably, each person experienced a deeper connection to themselves and the world. Most changed how they spent their time and money when they return to their daily lives. Participating in a program like mine helped people realize that an experience like the one we offered, brought them happiness, time to reflect on their lives, and plan for their futures.

It has been over 23 years since I took my first trip to Nepal. It is hard to put into words the beauty, the enchantment of the mountains and other sites in Nepal. The visceral experience of trekking, sitting with the children and parents in the village, seeing Nepalese women hoeing in their fields, carrying water, and caring for their children surrounded by the largest mountains in the world, while trekking, deepened my understanding of myself and tuned me into the sameness of other human beings. I'm happier and more joyful at this time in my life than

I've ever been before, because I combined my skills and experience to create a rewarding life in my sixties and seventies. You can too! Involvement in a culture that confronted my privileged Western views has been intensely liberating intellectually and emotionally, and has given me great joy and optimism for our future world.

By taking one step at a time and collaborating with people from different parts of the world, we've changed our lives and the lives of others. Our accomplishments have been successful and sustainable because of each person who has joined The Trek of Your Life, their generosity, warm-heartedness, and willingness to contribute their time, constructive ideas, a small monthly sum, and scholarships for the children. The rewards are indisputably long-lasting and two-way.

I hope my journey encourages you to combine your work experience and skills to create an activity or business that brings you joy and satisfaction in the years after 50. Maybe you can join me?

A frequently quoted message by Robert F. Kennedy Sr. is, "Let no one be discouraged by the belief there is nothing one person can do against the enormous array of the world's ills, misery, ignorance, and violence. Few will have the greatness to bend history, but each of us can work to change a small portion of events. And in the total of all those acts will be written the history of a generation."

We owe it to ourselves, our children, our grandchildren, and our world to add meaning, joy, and purpose to our lives. Our children are living in a polarized post-pandemic world, where digital social networks have the potential to generate a wave of change in a more complex world. I hope my experience will encourage you to contribute positively to a more communal, empathetic world.

Made in the USA
Columbia, SC
02 November 2023

25393695R00107